KB076019

Premium Voca

영어중심

숙어 & 속담

001
not A but B
A가 아니고 B이다

002
have to do with
~와 관련이 있다

003
in essence
본질적으로

004
in sum
요약하자면

005
on account of
~때문에

006
put an end to
~을 끝내다

007
on the basis of
~을 근거로 하여

008	
figure out	이해하다

009	
lay off	해고하다

010	
sort out	~을 분류하다

011	
be opposed to	~에 반대하다

012	
come of age	성년이 되다

013	
associated with	~와 관련된

014	
break up	해산하다

015	
be susceptible to	~의 영향을 받기 쉽다

016	
be derived from	~로부터 유래하다

017	
get around	돌아다니다

018	
first and foremost	무엇보다

019	
no sooner ~ than...	~하자마자 ...하다

020	
fill out	기입하다

021	
There is no use -ing	~해도 소용없다

Review Test

☑ 다음 숙어의 뜻을 우리말로 쓰시오.

01 break up _____   12 have to do with _____

02 be susceptible to _____   13 in essence _____

03 on the basis of _____   14 figure out _____

04 put an end to _____   15 first and foremost _____

05 come of age _____   16 There is no use -ing _____

06 lay off _____   17 get around _____

07 be opposed to _____   18 be derived from _____

08 associated with _____   19 on account of _____

09 no sooner ~ than... _____   20 not A but B _____

10 sort out _____   21 fill out _____

11 in sum _____

정답
01 해산하다
02 ~의 영향을 받기 쉽다
03 ~을 근거로 하여
04 ~을 끝내다
05 성년이 되다
06 해고하다
07 ~에 반대하다
08 ~와 관련된
09 ~하자마자 ...하다

10 ~을 분류하다
11 요약하자면
12 ~와 관련이 있다
13 본질적으로
14 이해하다
15 무엇보다
16 ~해도 소용없다
17 돌아다니다
18 ~로부터 유래하다

19 ~때문에
20 A가 아니고 B이다
21 기입하다

Review Test

☑ 다음 숙어의 뜻을 우리말로 쓰시오.

01 on account of _____

02 in sum _____

03 lay off _____

04 sort out _____

05 first and foremost _____

06 be opposed to _____

07 no sooner ~ than... _____

08 There is no use -ing _____

09 have to do with _____

10 come of age _____

11 associated with _____

12 put an end to _____

13 on the basis of _____

14 get around _____

15 be derived from _____

16 not A but B _____

17 in essence _____

18 be susceptible to _____

19 figure out _____

20 break up _____

21 fill out _____

정답
01 ~때문에	10 성년이 되다	19 이해하다
02 요약하자면	11 ~와 관련된	20 해산하다
03 해고하다	12 ~을 끝내다	21 기입하다
04 ~을 분류하다	13 ~을 근거로 하여	
05 무엇보다	14 돌아다니다	
06 ~에 반대하다	15 ~로부터 유래하다	
07 ~하자마자 ...하다	16 A가 아니고 B이다	
08 ~해도 소용없다	17 본질적으로	
09 ~와 관련이 있다	18 ~의 영향을 받기 쉽다	

Review Test

☑ 다음 숙어의 뜻을 우리말로 쓰시오.

01 in essence _____

02 put an end to _____

03 be susceptible to _____

04 figure out _____

05 on account of _____

06 come of age _____

07 be derived from _____

08 in sum _____

09 first and foremost _____

10 fill out _____

11 lay off _____

12 on the basis of _____

13 not A but B _____

14 sort out _____

15 have to do with _____

16 no sooner ~ than... _____

17 associated with _____

18 break up _____

19 get around _____

20 be opposed to _____

21 There is no use -ing _____

정답					
01 본질적으로	10 기입하다	19 돌아다니다
02 ~을 끝내다	11 해고하다	20 ~에 반대하다
03 ~의 영향을 받기 쉽다	12 ~을 근거로 하여	21 ~해도 소용없다
04 이해하다	13 A가 아니고 B이다	
05 ~때문에	14 ~을 분류하다	
06 성년이 되다	15 ~와 관련이 있다	
07 ~로부터 유래하다	16 ~하자마자 ...하다	
08 요약하자면	17 ~와 관련된	
09 무엇보다	18 해산하다	

022	in detail	자세히
023	live up to	~에 부응하다
024	look into	~을 조사하다
025	find out	알아내다
026	refer to	~을 언급하다
027	now and then	가끔
028	of itself	저절로

029	for the present	현재로서는
030	let down	실망시키다
031	bring up	~을 기르다
032	give A credit for B	A에게 B에 대한 공로를 인정하다
033	when it comes to	~에 관해서
034	break the record	기록을 깨다
035	take ~ into consideration	~을 고려하다

036	quite a few	꽤 많은
037	wear down	마모되다
038	instead of	~ 대신에
039	in order	순서대로
040	be willing to V	기꺼이 ~하다
041	block off	~을 막다
042	put ~ aside	~을 제쳐놓다

Review Test

☑ 다음 숙어의 뜻을 우리말로 쓰시오.

01 break the record	_____	12 let down	_____
02 give A credit for B	_____	13 now and then	_____
03 put ~ aside	_____	14 of itself	_____
04 take ~ into consideration	_____	15 be willing to V	_____
05 instead of	_____	16 look into	_____
06 for the present	_____	17 block off	_____
07 quite a few	_____	18 bring up	_____
08 in order	_____	19 wear down	_____
09 in detail	_____	20 find out	_____
10 refer to	_____	21 live up to	_____
11 when it comes to	_____		

정답
01 기록을 깨다
02 A에게 B에 대한 공로를 인정하다
03 ~을 제쳐놓다
04 ~을 고려하다
05 ~ 대신에
06 현재로서는
07 꽤 많은
08 순서대로
09 자세히
10 ~을 언급하다
11 ~에 관해서
12 실망시키다
13 가끔
14 저절로
15 기꺼이 ~하다
16 ~을 조사하다
17 ~을 막다
18 ~을 기르다
19 마모되다
20 알아내다
21 ~에 부응하다

Review Test

☑ 다음 숙어의 뜻을 우리말로 쓰시오.

01 block off _____

02 in order _____

03 bring up _____

04 in detail _____

05 now and then _____

06 for the present _____

07 instead of _____

08 look into _____

09 find out _____

10 give A credit for B _____

11 let down _____

12 wear down _____

13 when it comes to _____

14 quite a few _____

15 take ~ into consideration _____

16 live up to _____

17 put ~ aside _____

18 of itself _____

19 be willing to V _____

20 refer to _____

21 break the record _____

정답
01 ~을 막다	10 A에게 B에 대한 공로를 인정하다	19 기꺼이 ~하다
02 순서대로	11 실망시키다	20 ~을 언급하다
03 ~을 기르다	12 마모되다	21 기록을 깨다
04 자세히	13 ~에 관해서	
05 가끔	14 꽤 많은	
06 현재로서는	15 ~을 고려하다	
07 ~ 대신에	16 ~에 부응하다	
08 ~을 조사하다	17 ~을 제쳐놓다	
09 알아내다	18 저절로	

Review Test

☑ 다음 숙어의 뜻을 우리말로 쓰시오.

01 refer to _____

02 for the present _____

03 find out _____

04 take ~ into consideration _____

05 bring up _____

06 wear down _____

07 break the record _____

08 instead of _____

09 in order _____

10 now and then _____

11 quite a few _____

12 look into _____

13 in detail _____

14 of itself _____

15 put ~ aside _____

16 be willing to V _____

17 give A credit for B _____

18 live up to _____

19 let down _____

20 when it comes to _____

21 block off _____

정답			
01 ~을 언급하다	10 가끔	19 실망시키다
02 현재로서는	11 꽤 많은	20 ~에 관해서
03 알아내다	12 ~을 조사하다	21 ~을 막다
04 ~을 고려하다	13 자세히	
05 ~을 기르다	14 저절로	
06 마모되다	15 ~을 제쳐놓다	
07 기록을 깨다	16 기꺼이 ~하다	
08 ~ 대신에	17 A에게 B에 대한 공로를 인정하다	
09 순서대로	18 ~에 부응하다	

043
go bankrupt
파산하다

044
look forward to -ing
~을 기대하다

045
take pride in
~에 자부심을 갖다

046
strive to V
~하려고 노력하다

047
in the distance
멀리서

048
play a role
역할을 하다

049
turn to
~에 의존하다

050	
root out	~을 근절하다

051	
slip away	사라지다

052	
by and large	대체로

053	
turn down	~을 거절하다

054	
for the most part	대부분은

055	
what is called	이른바

056	
be capable of	~을 할 수 있다

057	
take responsibility for	~에 대해 책임을 지다

058	
be likely to V	~할 것 같다

059	
for the sake of	~을 위하여

060	
persist in	~을 주장하다

061	
attend to	~에 유의하다

062	
A such as B	B와 같은 A

063	
be good at	~을 잘하다

Review Test

☑ 다음 숙어의 뜻을 우리말로 쓰시오.

01 be good at	_____	12 take responsibility for	_____
02 for the sake of	_____	13 turn down	_____
03 turn to	_____	14 what is called	_____
04 be capable of	_____	15 in the distance	_____
05 strive to V	_____	16 play a role	_____
06 go bankrupt	_____	17 look forward to -ing	_____
07 A such as B	_____	18 be likely to V	_____
08 attend to	_____	19 take pride in	_____
09 by and large	_____	20 persist in	_____
10 slip away	_____	21 for the most part	_____
11 root out	_____		

정답
01 ~을 잘하다
02 ~을 위하여
03 ~에 의존하다
04 ~을 할 수 있다
05 ~하려고 노력하다
06 파산하다
07 B와 같은 A
08 ~에 유의하다
09 대체로

10 사라지다
11 ~을 근절하다
12 ~에 대해 책임을 지다
13 ~을 거절하다
14 이른바
15 멀리서
16 역할을 하다
17 ~을 기대하다
18 ~할 것 같다

19 ~에 자부심을 갖다
20 ~을 주장하다
21 대부분은

Review Test

☑ 다음 숙어의 뜻을 우리말로 쓰시오.

01 be capable of _____

02 go bankrupt _____

03 by and large _____

04 be likely to V _____

05 turn to _____

06 what is called _____

07 look forward to -ing _____

08 in the distance _____

09 attend to _____

10 take responsibility for _____

11 for the most part _____

12 root out _____

13 be good at _____

14 slip away _____

15 for the sake of _____

16 turn down _____

17 play a role _____

18 strive to V _____

19 take pride in _____

20 A such as B _____

21 persist in _____

Review Test

✓ 다음 숙어의 뜻을 우리말로 쓰시오.

01 root out _____

02 be capable of _____

03 persist in _____

04 slip away _____

05 strive to V _____

06 what is called _____

07 take responsibility for _____

08 play a role _____

09 turn to _____

10 for the most part _____

11 by and large _____

12 attend to _____

13 be good at _____

14 in the distance _____

15 turn down _____

16 go bankrupt _____

17 take pride in _____

18 for the sake of _____

19 be likely to V _____

20 look forward to -ing _____

21 A such as B _____

정답
01 ~을 근절하다
02 ~을 할 수 있다
03 ~을 주장하다
04 사라지다
05 ~하려고 노력하다
06 이른바
07 ~에 대해 책임을 지다
08 역할을 하다
09 ~에 의존하다

10 대부분은
11 대체로
12 ~에 유의하다
13 ~을 잘하다
14 멀리서
15 ~을 거절하다
16 파산하다
17 ~에 자부심을 갖다
18 ~을 위하여

19 ~할 것 같다
20 ~을 기대하다
21 B와 같은 A

064

stay up

자지 않고 일어나 있다

- - - - - - - - - - - - - - - - - - -

065

take charge of

~을 떠맡다

- - - - - - - - - - - - - - - - - - -

066

be concerned about

~에 대해 걱정하다

- - - - - - - - - - - - - - - - - - -

067

put down

~을 내려놓다

- - - - - - - - - - - - - - - - - - -

068

deprive A of B

A로부터 B를 빼앗다

- - - - - - - - - - - - - - - - - - -

069

pile up

쌓이다

- - - - - - - - - - - - - - - - - - -

070

aside from

~을 제외하고

- - - - - - - - - - - - - - - - - - -

071	set off	출발하다

072	break new ground	새 분야를 개척하다

073	irrespective of	~와 상관없이

074	to some degree	어느 정도

075	take account of	~을 고려하다

076	throw out	~을 버리다

077	be sold out	매진되다

078		
step by step		차근차근

079		
burst into		갑자기 ~하다

080		
have ~ in common		~을 공통점으로 가지고 있다

081		
break down		고장 나다

082		
build up		~을 축적하다

083		
bring about		~을 초래하다

084		
give ~ a hand		~에게 도움을 주다

Review Test

☑ 다음 숙어의 뜻을 우리말로 쓰시오.

01 break new ground _____   12 give ~ a hand _____

02 burst into _____   13 step by step _____

03 take charge of _____   14 set off _____

04 be concerned about _____   15 break down _____

05 bring about _____   16 take account of _____

06 stay up _____   17 pile up _____

07 aside from _____   18 irrespective of _____

08 put down _____   19 deprive A of B _____

09 to some degree _____   20 have ~ in common _____

10 be sold out _____   21 build up _____

11 throw out _____

정답

01 새 분야를 개척하다	10 매진되다	19 A로부터 B를 빼앗다
02 갑자기 ~하다	11 ~을 버리다	20 ~을 공통점으로 가지고 있다
03 ~을 떠맡다	12 ~에게 도움을 주다	21 ~을 축적하다
04 ~에 대해 걱정하다	13 차근차근	
05 ~을 초래하다	14 출발하다	
06 자지 않고 일어나 있다	15 고장 나다	
07 ~을 제외하고	16 ~을 고려하다	
08 ~을 내려놓다	17 쌓이다	
09 어느 정도	18 ~와 상관없이	

Review Test ————————————————————

☑ 다음 숙어의 뜻을 우리말로 쓰시오.

01 to some degree _____

02 give ~ a hand _____

03 have ~ in common _____

04 aside from _____

05 build up _____

06 take charge of _____

07 throw out _____

08 pile up _____

09 break new ground _____

10 deprive A of B _____

11 set off _____

12 be concerned about _____

13 break down _____

14 irrespective of _____

15 step by step _____

16 put down _____

17 stay up _____

18 take account of _____

19 be sold out _____

20 bring about _____

21 burst into _____

정답
01 어느 정도
02 ~에게 도움을 주다
03 ~을 공통점으로 가지고 있다
04 ~을 제외하고
05 ~을 축적하다
06 ~을 떠맡다
07 ~을 버리다
08 쌓이다
09 새 분야를 개척하다
10 A로부터 B를 빼앗다
11 출발하다
12 ~에 대해 걱정하다
13 고장 나다
14 ~와 상관없이
15 차근차근
16 ~을 내려놓다
17 자지 않고 일어나 있다
18 ~을 고려하다
19 매진되다
20 ~을 초래하다
21 갑자기 ~하다

Review Test

☑ 다음 숙어의 뜻을 우리말로 쓰시오.

01 have ~ in common _____

02 pile up _____

03 bring about _____

04 break new ground _____

05 break down _____

06 aside from _____

07 give ~ a hand _____

08 irrespective of _____

09 be sold out _____

10 take account of _____

11 deprive A of B _____

12 step by step _____

13 burst into _____

14 throw out _____

15 stay up _____

16 set off _____

17 take charge of _____

18 to some degree _____

19 put down _____

20 build up _____

21 be concerned about _____

정답 01 ~을 공통점으로 가지고 있다
02 쌓이다
03 ~을 초래하다
04 새 분야를 개척하다
05 고장 나다
06 ~을 제외하고
07 ~에게 도움을 주다
08 ~와 상관없이
09 매진되다

10 ~을 고려하다
11 A로부터 B를 빼앗다
12 차근차근
13 갑자기 ~하다
14 ~을 버리다
15 자지 않고 일어나 있다
16 출발하다
17 ~을 떠맡다
18 어느 정도

19 ~을 내려놓다
20 ~을 축적하다
21 ~에 대해 걱정하다

085	
substitute A for B	B를 A로 대체하다

086	
think over	심사숙고하다

087	
in public	공개적으로

088	
on occasion	가끔

089	
cut down on	~을 줄이다

090	
never ~ without -ing	~하면 반드시 -하다

091	
with respect to	~에 관하여

092	turn off	~을 끄다
093	give in	~에 굴복하다
094	make the point that	~라는 주장을 하다
095	set out on	착수하다
096	come by	~에 들르다
097	leave for	~을 향해 떠나다
098	call off	~을 취소하다

099	transform A into B	A를 B로 바꾸다

100	jump to conclusions	성급하게 결론을 내리다

101	a set of	일련의

102	take A to B	A를 B로 데려가다

103	be composed of	~로 구성되다

104	go over	~을 검토하다

105	hold back	~을 억누르다

Review Test

☑ 다음 숙어의 뜻을 우리말로 쓰시오.

01 come by _____

02 a set of _____

03 be composed of _____

04 call off _____

05 transform A into B _____

06 leave for _____

07 think over _____

08 hold back _____

09 make the point that _____

10 turn off _____

11 set out on _____

12 never ~ without -ing _____

13 on occasion _____

14 jump to conclusions _____

15 go over _____

16 give in _____

17 in public _____

18 take A to B _____

19 substitute A for B _____

20 cut down on _____

21 with respect to _____

정답
01 ~에 들르다
02 일련의
03 ~로 구성되다
04 ~을 취소하다
05 A를 B로 바꾸다
06 ~을 향해 떠나다
07 심사숙고하다
08 ~을 억누르다
09 ~라는 주장을 하다

10 ~을 끄다
11 착수하다
12 ~하면 반드시 -하다
13 가끔
14 성급하게 결론을 내리다
15 ~을 검토하다
16 ~에 굴복하다
17 공개적으로
18 A를 B로 데려가다

19 B를 A로 대체하다
20 ~을 줄이다
21 ~에 관하여

29

Review Test

☑ 다음 숙어의 뜻을 우리말로 쓰시오.

01 leave for _____

02 transform A into B _____

03 a set of _____

04 think over _____

05 take A to B _____

06 come by _____

07 set out on _____

08 call off _____

09 be composed of _____

10 cut down on _____

11 substitute A for B _____

12 jump to conclusions _____

13 give in _____

14 never ~ without -ing _____

15 hold back _____

16 in public _____

17 turn off _____

18 on occasion _____

19 make the point that _____

20 with respect to _____

21 go over _____

정답   01 ~을 향해 떠나다   10 ~을 줄이다   19 ~라는 주장을 하다
       02 A를 B로 바꾸다   11 B를 A로 대체하다   20 ~에 관하여
       03 일련의   12 성급하게 결론을 내리다 21 ~을 검토하다
       04 심사숙고하다   13 ~에 굴복하다
       05 A를 B로 데려가다   14 ~하면 반드시 -하다
       06 ~에 들르다   15 ~을 억누르다
       07 착수하다   16 공개적으로
       08 ~을 취소하다   17 ~을 끄다
       09 ~로 구성되다   18 가끔

Review Test

☑️ 다음 숙어의 뜻을 우리말로 쓰시오.

01 hold back _____ 12 think over _____

02 go over _____ 13 be composed of _____

03 cut down on _____ 14 never ~ without -ing _____

04 take A to B _____ 15 in public _____

05 make the point that _____ 16 come by _____

06 leave for _____ 17 a set of _____

07 transform A into B _____ 18 give in _____

08 substitute A for B _____ 19 on occasion _____

09 turn off _____ 20 set out on _____

10 with respect to _____ 21 jump to conclusions _____

11 call off _____

정답 01 ~을 억누르다   10 ~에 관하여   19 가끔
      02 ~을 검토하다   11 ~을 취소하다   20 착수하다
      03 ~을 줄이다   12 심사숙고하다   21 성급하게 결론을 내리다
      04 A를 B로 데려가다   13 ~로 구성되다
      05 ~라는 주장을 하다   14 ~하면 반드시 -하다
      06 ~을 향해 떠나다   15 공개적으로
      07 A를 B로 바꾸다   16 ~에 들르다
      08 B를 A로 대체하다   17 일련의
      09 ~을 끄다   18 ~에 굴복하다

106	
on one's behalf	~을 대신하여

107	
regardless of	~에 상관없이

108	
go away	떠나다

109	
on top of	~외에

110	
in the light of	~의 관점에서

111	
under consideration	고려 중인

112	
be stuck in	~에 갇히다

113 devote oneself to	~에 전념하다
114 pass away	죽다
115 specialize in	~을 전공하다
116 run for	~에 출마하다
117 on time	정각에
118 stay away from	~을 가까이하지 않다
119 attribute A to B	A를 B의 탓이라고 하다

120	at random	무작위로
121	at risk	위험한
122	put up with	~을 참다
123	adhere to	~을 충실히 지키다
124	hold down	~을 억제하다
125	come down with	(질병)에 걸리다
126	keep in mind	~을 명심하다

Review Test

☑ 다음 숙어의 뜻을 우리말로 쓰시오.

01 go away	_____	12 in the light of	_____
02 on time	_____	13 keep in mind	_____
03 at risk	_____	14 on one's behalf	_____
04 adhere to	_____	15 put up with	_____
05 hold down	_____	16 attribute A to B	_____
06 under consideration	_____	17 run for	_____
07 at random	_____	18 specialize in	_____
08 on top of	_____	19 regardless of	_____
09 be stuck in	_____	20 come down with	_____
10 devote oneself to	_____	21 pass away	_____
11 stay away from	_____		

정답
01 떠나다	10 ~에 전념하다	19 ~에 상관없이
02 정각에	11 ~을 가까이하지 않다	20 (질병)에 걸리다
03 위험한	12 ~의 관점에서	21 죽다
04 ~을 충실히 지키다	13 ~을 명심하다	
05 ~을 억제하다	14 ~을 대신하여	
06 고려 중인	15 ~을 참다	
07 무작위로	16 A를 B의 탓이라고 하다	
08 ~외에	17 ~에 출마하다	
09 ~에 갇히다	18 ~을 전공하다	

Review Test

☑ 다음 숙어의 뜻을 우리말로 쓰시오.

01 in the light of _____

02 put up with _____

03 attribute A to B _____

04 come down with _____

05 on one's behalf _____

06 devote oneself to _____

07 go away _____

08 hold down _____

09 at random _____

10 on time _____

11 under consideration _____

12 on top of _____

13 pass away _____

14 stay away from _____

15 adhere to _____

16 regardless of _____

17 be stuck in _____

18 at risk _____

19 keep in mind _____

20 specialize in _____

21 run for _____

정답

01 ~의 관점에서	10 정각에	19 ~을 명심하다
02 ~을 참다	11 고려 중인	20 ~을 전공하다
03 A를 B의 탓이라고 하다	12 ~외에	21 ~에 출마하다
04 (질병)에 걸리다	13 죽다	
05 ~을 대신하여	14 ~을 가까이하지 않다	
06 ~에 전념하다	15 ~을 충실히 지키다	
07 떠나다	16 ~에 상관없이	
08 ~을 억제하다	17 ~에 갇히다	
09 무작위로	18 위험한	

Review Test

☑ 다음 숙어의 뜻을 우리말로 쓰시오.

01 on time _____

02 put up with _____

03 hold down _____

04 attribute A to B _____

05 at random _____

06 stay away from _____

07 regardless of _____

08 keep in mind _____

09 specialize in _____

10 devote oneself to _____

11 run for _____

12 under consideration _____

13 on top of _____

14 at risk _____

15 come down with _____

16 pass away _____

17 go away _____

18 adhere to _____

19 on one's behalf _____

20 in the light of _____

21 be stuck in _____

정답
01 정각에	10 ~에 전념하다	19 ~을 대신하여
02 ~을 참다	11 ~에 출마하다	20 ~의 관점에서
03 ~을 억제하다	12 고려 중인	21 ~에 갇히다
04 A를 B의 탓이라고 하다	13 ~외에	
05 무작위로	14 위험한	
06 ~을 가까이하지 않다	15 (질병)에 걸리다	
07 ~에 상관없이	16 죽다	
08 ~을 명심하다	17 떠나다	
09 ~을 전공하다	18 ~을 충실히 지키다	

127	in progress	진행 중인
128	on board	탑승한
129	date back to	~로 거슬러 올라가다
130	use up	다 써 버리다
131	prior to	~의 전에
132	be concerned with	~와 관련이 있다
133	accuse A of B	A를 B로 고소하다

134	not to mention	~은 말할 것도 없고
135	in succession	연속으로
136	insist on	~을 주장하다
137	turn around	방향을 바꾸다
138	inform A of B	A에게 B를 알리다
139	look up to	~을 존경하다
140	be loaded with	~로 가득 차다

141	
in place of	~대신에

142	
get used to 명사(-ing)	~에 익숙해지다

143	
above all	무엇보다도

144	
as opposed to	~와는 대조적으로

145	
gather around	모이다

146	
take out	~을 꺼내다

147	
make use of	~을 이용하다

Review Test

☑ 다음 숙어의 뜻을 우리말로 쓰시오.

01 be loaded with	_____	12 on board	_____
02 in place of	_____	13 date back to	_____
03 accuse A of B	_____	14 not to mention	_____
04 be concerned with	_____	15 as opposed to	_____
05 inform A of B	_____	16 make use of	_____
06 in succession	_____	17 above all	_____
07 turn around	_____	18 get used to 명사(-ing)	_____
08 look up to	_____	19 prior to	_____
09 gather around	_____	20 in progress	_____
10 insist on	_____	21 take out	_____
11 use up	_____		

정답

01 ~로 가득 차다	10 ~을 주장하다	19 ~의 전에
02 ~대신에	11 다 써 버리다	20 진행 중인
03 A를 B로 고소하다	12 탑승한	21 ~을 꺼내다
04 ~와 관련이 있다	13 ~로 거슬러 올라가다	
05 A에게 B를 알리다	14 ~은 말할 것도 없고	
06 연속으로	15 ~와는 대조적으로	
07 방향을 바꾸다	16 ~을 이용하다	
08 ~을 존경하다	17 무엇보다도	
09 모이다	18 ~에 익숙해지다	

Review Test

☑ 다음 숙어의 뜻을 우리말로 쓰시오.

01 prior to _____   12 be concerned with _____

02 use up _____   13 accuse A of B _____

03 in succession _____   14 above all _____

04 insist on _____   15 get used to 명사(-ing) _____

05 as opposed to _____   16 in progress _____

06 turn around _____   17 date back to _____

07 gather around _____   18 in place of _____

08 make use of _____   19 not to mention _____

09 on board _____   20 be loaded with _____

10 inform A of B _____   21 take out _____

11 look up to _____

정답 01 ~의 전에   10 A에게 B를 알리다   19 ~은 말할 것도 없고
      02 다 써 버리다   11 ~을 존경하다   20 ~로 가득 차다
      03 연속으로   12 ~와 관련이 있다   21 ~을 꺼내다
      04 ~을 주장하다   13 A를 B로 고소하다
      05 ~와는 대조적으로   14 무엇보다도
      06 방향을 바꾸다   15 ~에 익숙해지다
      07 모이다   16 진행 중인
      08 ~을 이용하다   17 ~로 거슬러 올라가다
      09 탑승한   18 ~대신에

42

Review Test

☑ 다음 숙어의 뜻을 우리말로 쓰시오.

01 date back to _____   12 accuse A of B _____

02 be concerned with _____   13 in progress _____

03 in place of _____   14 insist on _____

04 not to mention _____   15 on board _____

05 prior to _____   16 gather around _____

06 inform A of B _____   17 look up to _____

07 get used to 명사(-ing) _____   18 be loaded with _____

08 use up _____   19 above all _____

09 as opposed to _____   20 turn around _____

10 take out _____   21 make use of _____

11 in succession _____

정답
01 ~로 거슬러 올라가다   10 ~을 꺼내다   19 무엇보다도
02 ~와 관련이 있다   11 연속으로   20 방향을 바꾸다
03 ~대신에   12 A를 B로 고소하다   21 ~을 이용하다
04 ~은 말할 것도 없고   13 진행 중인
05 ~의 전에   14 ~을 주장하다
06 A에게 B를 알리다   15 탑승한
07 ~에 익숙해지다   16 모이다
08 다 써 버리다   17 ~을 존경하다
09 ~와는 대조적으로   18 ~로 가득 차다

148
think of A as B

A를 B로 여기다

149
catch a cold

감기에 걸리다

150
engage in

~에 참여하다

151
be sick of

~에 싫증이 나다

152
look on A as B

A를 B로 여기다

153
if anything

오히려

154
by virtue of

~덕분에

155	consist in	~에 있다
156	be packed with	~로 가득 차다
157	make a living	생계를 꾸려가다
158	end up -ing	결국 ~하게되다
159	long for	~을 갈망하다
160	far from	전혀 ~이 아닌
161	be devoid of	~이 없다

162 put off	~을 미루다
163 catch up with	~을 따라잡다
164 stick with	~을 계속하다
165 mess up	~을 망치다
166 be supposed to V	~하기로 되어 있다
167 prevent A from B(-ing)	A가 B하는 것을 막다
168 get away	~을 벗어나다

Review Test

☑ 다음 숙어의 뜻을 우리말로 쓰시오.

01 far from	_____	12 be packed with	_____
02 end up -ing	_____	13 if anything	_____
03 get away	_____	14 by virtue of	_____
04 be devoid of	_____	15 be supposed to V	_____
05 stick with	_____	16 engage in	_____
06 consist in	_____	17 prevent A from B(-ing)	_____
07 put off	_____	18 make a living	_____
08 mess up	_____	19 catch up with	_____
09 think of A as B	_____	20 look on A as B	_____
10 be sick of	_____	21 catch a cold	_____
11 long for	_____		

정답

01 전혀 ~이 아닌	10 ~에 싫증이 나다	19 ~을 따라잡다
02 결국 ~하게되다	11 ~을 갈망하다	20 A를 B로 여기다
03 ~을 벗어나다	12 ~로 가득 차다	21 감기에 걸리다
04 ~이 없다	13 오히려	
05 ~을 계속하다	14 ~덕분에	
06 ~에 있다	15 ~하기로 되어 있다	
07 ~을 미루다	16 ~에 참여하다	
08 ~을 망치다	17 A가 B하는 것을 막다	
09 A를 B로 여기다	18 생계를 꾸려가다	

47

Review Test

☑ 다음 숙어의 뜻을 우리말로 쓰시오.

01 be devoid of _____

02 be supposed to V _____

03 prevent A from B(-ing) _____

04 make a living _____

05 think of A as B _____

06 end up -ing _____

07 stick with _____

08 long for _____

09 mess up _____

10 engage in _____

11 look on A as B _____

12 if anything _____

13 by virtue of _____

14 be sick of _____

15 far from _____

16 catch a cold _____

17 put off _____

18 get away _____

19 be packed with _____

20 catch up with _____

21 consist in _____

정답
01 ~이 없다
02 ~하기로 되어 있다
03 A가 B하는 것을 막다
04 생계를 꾸려가다
05 A를 B로 여기다
06 결국 ~하게되다
07 ~을 계속하다
08 ~을 갈망하다
09 ~을 망치다
10 ~에 참여하다
11 A를 B로 여기다
12 오히려
13 ~덕분에
14 ~에 싫증이 나다
15 전혀 ~이 아닌
16 감기에 걸리다
17 ~을 미루다
18 ~을 벗어나다
19 ~로 가득 차다
20 ~을 따라잡다
21 ~에 있다

Review Test

다음 숙어의 뜻을 우리말로 쓰시오.

01 look on A as B ....

02 consist in ....

03 be sick of ....

04 be devoid of ....

05 make a living ....

06 catch up with ....

07 far from ....

08 stick with ....

09 mess up ....

10 if anything ....

11 put off ....

12 engage in ....

13 think of A as B ....

14 by virtue of ....

15 get away ....

16 be supposed to V ....

17 end up -ing ....

18 catch a cold ....

19 be packed with ....

20 long for ....

21 prevent A from B(-ing) ....

정답
01 A를 B로 여기다
02 ~에 있다
03 ~에 싫증이 나다
04 ~이 없다
05 생계를 꾸려가다
06 ~을 따라잡다
07 전혀 ~이 아닌
08 ~을 계속하다
09 ~을 망치다

10 오히려
11 ~을 미루다
12 ~에 참여하다
13 A를 B로 여기다
14 ~덕분에
15 ~을 벗어나다
16 ~하기로 되어 있다
17 결국 ~하게되다
18 감기에 걸리다

19 ~로 가득 차다
20 ~을 갈망하다
21 A가 B하는 것을 막다

169	
on and on	계속해서

170	
on the whole	대체로

171	
be conscious of	~을 의식하다

172	
translate A into B	A를 B로 번역하다

173	
try on	입어 보다

174	
come out of	~에서 나오다

175	
at the cost of	~을 희생하여

176	
get over	~을 극복하다

177	
take the place of	~을 대신하다

178	
in search of	~을 찾아서

179	
once in a while	가끔

180	
on the spot	즉석에서

181	
due to	~때문에

182	
hang up	전화를 끊다

183	
in one's place	~의 대신에

184	
deal with	~을 처리하다

185	
over and over	반복해서

186	
the + 비교급 ~, the + 비교급	~하면 할수록 더 ~하다

187	
next to	거의

188	
crash into	~와 부딪치다

189	
be credited with	~로 공로를 인정받다

Review Test

☑ 다음 숙어의 뜻을 우리말로 쓰시오.

01 take the place of	_____	12 be conscious of	_____
02 deal with	_____	13 once in a while	_____
03 the + 비교급 ~, the + 비교급	_____	14 come out of	_____
04 hang up	_____	15 get over	_____
05 in search of	_____	16 crash into	_____
06 at the cost of	_____	17 on the whole	_____
07 in one's place	_____	18 next to	_____
08 be credited with	_____	19 over and over	_____
09 try on	_____	20 on the spot	_____
10 on and on	_____	21 translate A into B	_____
11 due to	_____		

정답
01 ~을 대신하다	10 계속해서	19 반복해서
02 ~을 처리하다	11 ~때문에	20 즉석에서
03 ~하면 할수록 더 ~하다	12 ~을 의식하다	21 A를 B로 번역하다
04 전화를 끊다	13 가끔	
05 ~을 찾아서	14 ~에서 나오다	
06 ~을 희생하여	15 ~을 극복하다	
07 ~의 대신에	16 ~와 부딪치다	
08 ~로 공로를 인정받다	17 대체로	
09 입어 보다	18 거의	

Review Test ───────────

☑ 다음 숙어의 뜻을 우리말로 쓰시오.

01 be credited with	_____	12 in one's place	_____
02 over and over	_____	13 once in a while	_____
03 at the cost of	_____	14 due to	_____
04 hang up	_____	15 try on	_____
05 translate A into B	_____	16 come out of	_____
06 on and on	_____	17 on the whole	_____
07 crash into	_____	18 deal with	_____
08 next to	_____	19 be conscious of	_____
09 in search of	_____	20 the + 비교급 ~, the + 비교급	_____
10 take the place of	_____	21 on the spot	_____
11 get over	_____		

정답
01 ~로 공로를 인정받다	10 ~을 대신하다	19 ~을 의식하다
02 반복해서	11 ~을 극복하다	20 ~하면 할수록 더 ~하다
03 ~을 희생하여	12 ~의 대신에	21 즉석에서
04 전화를 끊다	13 가끔	
05 A를 B로 번역하다	14 ~때문에	
06 계속해서	15 입어 보다	
07 ~와 부딪치다	16 ~에서 나오다	
08 거의	17 대체로	
09 ~을 찾아서	18 ~을 처리하다	

Review Test

☑ 다음 숙어의 뜻을 우리말로 쓰시오.

01 hang up   12 get over

02 on and on   13 be credited with

03 in search of   14 take the place of

04 deal with   15 over and over

05 at the cost of   16 once in a while

06 due to   17 come out of

07 on the whole   18 translate A into B

08 try on   19 be conscious of

09 next to   20 crash into

10 in one's place   21 the + 비교급 ~, the + 비교급

11 on the spot

정답

01 전화를 끊다	10 ~의 대신에	19 ~을 의식하다
02 계속해서	11 즉석에서	20 ~와 부딪치다
03 ~을 찾아서	12 ~을 극복하다	21 ~하면 할수록 더 ~하다
04 ~을 처리하다	13 ~로 공로를 인정받다	
05 ~을 희생하여	14 ~을 대신하다	
06 ~때문에	15 반복해서	
07 대체로	16 가끔	
08 입어 보다	17 ~에서 나오다	
09 거의	18 A를 B로 번역하다	

190		
in the meantime		그 동안

191		
be bound to V		반드시 ~해야 하다

192		
run short		부족하다

193		
take a course		강의를 듣다

194		
on the grounds that		~라는 이유로

195		
hold one's breath		숨을 멈추다

196		
be aware of		~을 알다

197	a great deal of	많은
198	provide A with B	A에게 B를 공급하다
199	get together	모이다
200	know A from B	A와 B를 구별하다
201	come across	~을 우연히 만나다
202	to the full	충분히
203	on purpose	고의로

204	anything but	결코 ~은 아닌

205	turn over	~을 뒤집다

206	pay attention to	~에 주목하다

207	as usual	평소와 같이

208	take in	~을 섭취하다

209	rely on	~에 의존하다

210	be compelled to V	어쩔 수 없이 ~하다

Review Test

☑ 다음 숙어의 뜻을 우리말로 쓰시오.

01 a great deal of _____   12 take in _____

02 on purpose _____   13 be compelled to V _____

03 as usual _____   14 on the grounds that _____

04 provide A with B _____   15 know A from B _____

05 take a course _____   16 in the meantime _____

06 to the full _____   17 run short _____

07 anything but _____   18 pay attention to _____

08 hold your breath _____   19 turn over _____

09 be aware of _____   20 be bound to V _____

10 come across _____   21 rely on _____

11 get together _____

정답
01 많은	10 ~을 우연히 만나다	19 ~을 뒤집다
02 고의로	11 모이다	20 반드시 ~해야 하다
03 평소와 같이	12 ~을 섭취하다	21 ~에 의존하다
04 A에게 B를 공급하다	13 어쩔 수 없이 ~하다	
05 강의를 듣다	14 ~라는 이유로	
06 충분히	15 A와 B를 구별하다	
07 결코 ~은 아닌	16 그 동안	
08 숨을 멈추다	17 부족하다	
09 ~을 알다	18 ~에 주목하다	

Review Test

☑ 다음 숙어의 뜻을 우리말로 쓰시오.

01 provide A with B _____

02 turn over _____

03 be bound to V _____

04 run short _____

05 rely on _____

06 in the meantime _____

07 be aware of _____

08 take a course _____

09 know A from B _____

10 on purpose _____

11 to the full _____

12 be compelled to V _____

13 anything but _____

14 a great deal of _____

15 as usual _____

16 come across _____

17 hold your breath _____

18 get together _____

19 on the grounds that _____

20 pay attention to _____

21 take in _____

정답   01 A에게 B를 공급하다   10 고의로   19 ~라는 이유로
       02 ~을 뒤집다   11 충분히   20 ~에 주목하다
       03 반드시 ~해야 하다   12 어쩔 수 없이 ~하다   21 ~을 섭취하다
       04 부족하다   13 결코 ~은 아닌
       05 ~에 의존하다   14 많은
       06 그 동안   15 평소와 같이
       07 ~을 알다   16 ~을 우연히 만나다
       08 강의를 듣다   17 숨을 멈추다
       09 A와 B를 구별하다   18 모이다

Review Test

☑ 다음 숙어의 뜻을 우리말로 쓰시오.

01 know A from B	_____	12 run short	_____
02 be compelled to V	_____	13 as usual	_____
03 pay attention to	_____	14 get together	_____
04 be aware of	_____	15 anything but	_____
05 take in	_____	16 take a course	_____
06 be bound to V	_____	17 in the meantime	_____
07 to the full	_____	18 come across	_____
08 hold your breath	_____	19 on purpose	_____
09 provide A with B	_____	20 rely on	_____
10 on the grounds that	_____	21 turn over	_____
11 a great deal of	_____		

정답
01 A와 B를 구별하다	10 ~라는 이유로	19 고의로
02 어쩔 수 없이 ~하다	11 많은	20 ~에 의존하다
03 ~에 주목하다	12 부족하다	21 ~을 뒤집다
04 ~을 알다	13 평소와 같이	
05 ~을 섭취하다	14 모이다	
06 반드시 ~해야 하다	15 결코 ~은 아닌	
07 충분히	16 강의를 듣다	
08 숨을 멈추다	17 그 동안	
09 A에게 B를 공급하다	18 ~을 우연히 만나다	

| 211 | last but not least | 마지막으로 |

| 212 | on -ing | ~하자마자 |

| 213 | discourage A from B(-ing) | A가 B하지 못하게 단념시키다 |

| 214 | fall back | 물러나다 |

| 215 | manage to V | 가까스로 ~하다 |

| 216 | dwell on | ~에 대해 깊게 생각하다 |

| 217 | take action | 조치를 취하다 |

218	make the most of	~을 최대한 활용하다
219	be forced to V	~하지 않을 수 없다
220	with regard to	~에 관하여
221	give up	~을 포기하다
222	cheer up	~을 격려하다
223	in some respects	어떤 점에서
224	take away	~을 빼앗다

225	take one's time	천천히 하다
226	prefer A to B	B보다 A를 더 좋아하다
227	fall behind	뒤처지다
228	depending upon	~에 따라
229	but for	~가 없으면
230	see off	~을 배웅하다
231	turn up	소리를 크게 하다

Review Test

☑️ 다음 숙어의 뜻을 우리말로 쓰시오.

01 fall behind _____

02 dwell on _____

03 see off _____

04 be forced to V _____

05 depending upon _____

06 take action _____

07 turn up _____

08 with regard to _____

09 take away _____

10 cheer up _____

11 manage to V _____

12 take one's time _____

13 prefer A to B _____

14 in some respects _____

15 last but not least _____

16 make the most of _____

17 on -ing _____

18 give up _____

19 fall back _____

20 but for _____

21 discourage A from B(-ing) _____

정답
01 뒤처지다	10 ~을 격려하다	19 물러나다
02 ~에 대해 깊게 생각하다	11 가까스로 ~하다	20 ~가 없으면
03 ~을 배웅하다	12 천천히 하다	21 A가 B하지 못하게 단념시키다
04 ~하지 않을 수 없다	13 B보다 A를 더 좋아하다	
05 ~에 따라	14 어떤 점에서	
06 조치를 취하다	15 마지막으로	
07 소리를 크게 하다	16 ~을 최대한 활용하다	
08 ~에 관하여	17 ~하자마자	
09 ~을 빼앗다	18 ~을 포기하다	

Review Test ———————————

☑ 다음 숙어의 뜻을 우리말로 쓰시오.

01 fall back _____

02 dwell on _____

03 fall behind _____

04 turn up _____

05 last but not least _____

06 see off _____

07 take away _____

08 make the most of _____

09 be forced to V _____

10 depending upon _____

11 take action _____

12 give up _____

13 in some respects _____

14 prefer A to B _____

15 discourage A from B(-ing) _____

16 take one's time _____

17 but for _____

18 with regard to _____

19 on -ing _____

20 cheer up _____

21 manage to V _____

정답
01 물러나다	10 ~에 따라	19 ~하자마자
02 ~에 대해 깊게 생각하다	11 조치를 취하다	20 ~을 격려하다
03 뒤처지다	12 ~을 포기하다	21 가까스로 ~하다
04 소리를 크게 하다	13 어떤 점에서	
05 마지막으로	14 B보다 A를 더 좋아하다	
06 ~을 배웅하다	15 A가 B하지 못하게 단념시키다	
07 ~을 빼앗다	16 천천히 하다	
08 ~을 최대한 활용하다	17 ~가 없으면	
09 ~하지 않을 수 없다	18 ~에 관하여	

Review Test

☑ 다음 숙어의 뜻을 우리말로 쓰시오.

01 cheer up _____   12 dwell on _____

02 fall behind _____   13 fall back _____

03 but for _____   14 prefer A to B _____

04 take away _____   15 see off _____

05 take one's time _____   16 be forced to V _____

06 in some respects _____   17 discourage A from B(-ing) _____

07 on -ing _____   18 depending upon _____

08 turn up _____   19 last but not least _____

09 with regard to _____   20 manage to V _____

10 make the most of _____   21 take action _____

11 give up _____

정답

01 ~을 격려하다	10 ~을 최대한 활용하다	19 마지막으로
02 뒤처지다	11 ~을 포기하다	20 가까스로 ~하다
03 ~가 없으면	12 ~에 대해 깊게 생각하다	21 조치를 취하다
04 ~을 빼앗다	13 물러나다	
05 천천히 하다	14 B보다 A를 더 좋아하다	
06 어떤 점에서	15 ~을 배웅하다	
07 ~하자마자	16 ~하지 않을 수 없다	
08 소리를 크게 하다	17 A가 B하지 못하게 단념시키다	
09 ~에 관하여	18 ~에 따라	

DAY 12 숙어

232 as it is	있는 그대로
233 be fed up with	~에 질리다
234 reflect on	깊이 생각하다
235 in terms of	~의 측면에서
236 after all	결국
237 can't help but V	~하지 않을 수 없다
238 wipe out	~을 완전히 없애 버리다

239	
set aside	~을 제쳐 놓다

240	
for ages	오랫동안

241	
replace A with B	A를 B로 대체하다

242	
in effect	사실상

243	
in haste	서둘러

244	
be associated with	~와 관련이 있다

245	
eat out	외식하다

246	
at a loss	당황하여

247	
no more than	단지

248	
stand for	~을 나타내다

249	
make up for	~을 보충하다

250	
may well V	~하는 것도 당연하다

251	
cut back on	~을 줄이다

252	
go for	~에 찬성하다

Review Test

☑️ 다음 숙어의 뜻을 우리말로 쓰시오.

01 be associated with _____   12 no more than _____

02 at a loss _____   13 for ages _____

03 stand for _____   14 can't help but V _____

04 be fed up with _____   15 go for _____

05 make up for _____   16 reflect on _____

06 in haste _____   17 set aside _____

07 in effect _____   18 in terms of _____

08 eat out _____   19 replace A with B _____

09 may well V _____   20 wipe out _____

10 after all _____   21 cut back on _____

11 as it is _____

정답
01 ~와 관련이 있다	10 결국	19 A를 B로 대체하다
02 당황하여	11 있는 그대로	20 ~을 완전히 없애 버리다
03 ~을 나타내다	12 단지	21 ~을 줄이다
04 ~에 질리다	13 오랫동안	
05 ~을 보충하다	14 ~하지 않을 수 없다	
06 서둘러	15 ~에 찬성하다	
07 사실상	16 깊이 생각하다	
08 외식하다	17 ~을 제쳐 놓다	
09 ~하는 것도 당연하다	18 ~의 측면에서	

Review Test

☑ 다음 숙어의 뜻을 우리말로 쓰시오.

01 go for _____   12 be fed up with _____

02 cut back on _____   13 may well V _____

03 after all _____   14 can't help but V _____

04 make up for _____   15 reflect on _____

05 replace A with B _____   16 in haste _____

06 be associated with _____   17 stand for _____

07 at a loss _____   18 for ages _____

08 as it is _____   19 in terms of _____

09 set aside _____   20 in effect _____

10 wipe out _____   21 no more than _____

11 eat out _____

정답
01 ~에 찬성하다	10 ~을 완전히 없애 버리다	19 ~의 측면에서
02 ~을 줄이다	11 외식하다	20 사실상
03 결국	12 ~에 질리다	21 단지
04 ~을 보충하다	13 ~하는 것도 당연하다	
05 A를 B로 대체하다	14 ~하지 않을 수 없다	
06 ~와 관련이 있다	15 깊이 생각하다	
07 당황하여	16 서둘러	
08 있는 그대로	17 ~을 나타내다	
09 ~을 제쳐 놓다	18 오랫동안	

Review Test

☑ 다음 숙어의 뜻을 우리말로 쓰시오.

01 reflect on _____

02 in haste _____

03 no more than _____

04 make up for _____

05 may well V _____

06 can't help but V _____

07 at a loss _____

08 in terms of _____

09 wipe out _____

10 set aside _____

11 be associated with _____

12 after all _____

13 go for _____

14 as it is _____

15 stand for _____

16 eat out _____

17 in effect _____

18 replace A with B _____

19 be fed up with _____

20 cut back on _____

21 for ages _____

정답			
01 깊이 생각하다	10 ~을 제쳐 놓다	19 ~에 질리다
02 서둘러	11 ~와 관련이 있다	20 ~을 줄이다
03 단지	12 결국	21 오랫동안
04 ~을 보충하다	13 ~에 찬성하다	
05 ~하는 것도 당연하다	14 있는 그대로	
06 ~하지 않을 수 없다	15 ~을 나타내다	
07 당황하여	16 외식하다	
08 ~의 측면에서	17 사실상	
09 ~을 완전히 없애 버리다	18 A를 B로 대체하다	

253	
pop up	갑자기 생기다

254	
at any rate	어쨌든

255	
hold on	~을 기다리다

256	
by accident	우연히

257	
for oneself	혼자 힘으로

258	
in vain	헛되이

259	
be content with	~에 만족하다

260	on behalf of	~을 대표하여
261	be occupied in	~에 전념하다
262	in question	논의가 되고 있는
263	cut in	끼어들다
264	at all costs	무슨 수를 써서라도
265	in turn	결과적으로
266	cannot help -ing	~하지 않을 수 없다

267	
free of	~이 없는

268	
around the corner	임박한

269	
be inclined to V	~하는 경향이 있다

270	
by oneself	혼자서

271	
be about to V	막 ~하려고 하다

272	
spring from	~에서 생겨나다

273	
in the face of	~에 직면하여

Review Test

☑ 다음 숙어의 뜻을 우리말로 쓰시오.

01 for oneself	_____	12 by accident	_____
02 be inclined to V	_____	13 be occupied in	_____
03 cannot help -ing	_____	14 in turn	_____
04 spring from	_____	15 by oneself	_____
05 pop up	_____	16 at any rate	_____
06 on behalf of	_____	17 be content with	_____
07 hold on	_____	18 around the corner	_____
08 be about to V	_____	19 in the face of	_____
09 free of	_____	20 in question	_____
10 at all costs	_____	21 cut in	_____
11 in vain	_____		

정답
01 혼자 힘으로	10 무슨 수를 써서라도	19 ~에 직면하여
02 ~하는 경향이 있다	11 헛되이	20 논의가 되고 있는
03 ~하지 않을 수 없다	12 우연히	21 끼어들다
04 ~에서 생겨나다	13 ~에 전념하다	
05 갑자기 생기다	14 결과적으로	
06 ~을 대표하여	15 혼자서	
07 ~을 기다리다	16 어쨌든	
08 막 ~하려고 하다	17 ~에 만족하다	
09 ~이 없는	18 임박한	

Review Test

☑ 다음 숙어의 뜻을 우리말로 쓰시오.

01 at all costs _____ 12 cut in _____

02 around the corner _____ 13 hold on _____

03 free of _____ 14 on behalf of _____

04 be inclined to V _____ 15 be content with _____

05 in turn _____ 16 spring from _____

06 at any rate _____ 17 in question _____

07 be occupied in _____ 18 for oneself _____

08 be about to V _____ 19 in the face of _____

09 cannot help -ing _____ 20 by accident _____

10 in vain _____ 21 pop up _____

11 by oneself _____

정답
01 무슨 수를 써서라도	10 헛되이	19 ~에 직면하여
02 임박한	11 혼자서	20 우연히
03 ~이 없는	12 끼어들다	21 갑자기 생기다
04 ~하는 경향이 있다	13 ~을 기다리다	
05 결과적으로	14 ~을 대표하여	
06 어쨌든	15 ~에 만족하다	
07 ~에 전념하다	16 ~에서 생겨나다	
08 막 ~하려고 하다	17 논의가 되고 있는	
09 ~하지 않을 수 없다	18 혼자 힘으로	

Review Test

☑️ 다음 숙어의 뜻을 우리말로 쓰시오.

01 cannot help -ing		12 at any rate	
02 free of		13 hold on	
03 be content with		14 on behalf of	
04 in vain		15 by oneself	
05 at all costs		16 in the face of	
06 be occupied in		17 be inclined to V	
07 cut in		18 around the corner	
08 in turn		19 for oneself	
09 be about to V		20 pop up	
10 in question		21 spring from	
11 by accident			

정답

01 ~하지 않을 수 없다	10 논의가 되고 있는	19 혼자 힘으로
02 ~이 없는	11 우연히	20 갑자기 생기다
03 ~에 만족하다	12 어쨌든	21 ~에서 생겨나다
04 헛되이	13 ~을 기다리다	
05 무슨 수를 써서라도	14 ~을 대표하여	
06 ~에 전념하다	15 혼자서	
07 끼어들다	16 ~에 직면하여	
08 결과적으로	17 ~하는 경향이 있다	
09 막 ~하려고 하다	18 임박한	

274	
back and forth	앞뒤로

275	
show off	과시하다

276	
rule out	~을 제외하다

277	
side by side	나란히

278	
in the presence of	~가 있을 때에는

279	
without regard to	~에 상관없이

280	
be marked by	~라는 특징을 갖다

281 put on	~을 입다
282 make up	~을 구성하다
283 hand in	~을 제출하다
284 be accustomed to 명사(-ing)	~하는 데 익숙하다
285 frankly speaking	솔직히 말해서
286 not so much A as B	A라기 보다는 오히려 B
287 so to speak	말하자면

288	resort to	~에 의존하다

289	regard A as B	A를 B로 여기다

290	look up	~을 찾다

291	allow for	~을 가능하게 하다

292	may as well V	~하는 것이 낫다

293	be endowed with	~을 부여받다

294	keep away from	~을 멀리하다

Review Test

☑️ 다음 숙어의 뜻을 우리말로 쓰시오.

01 in the presence of _____

02 side by side _____

03 make up _____

04 hand in _____

05 allow for _____

06 be accustomed to 명사(-ing) _____

07 may as well V _____

08 keep away from _____

09 show off _____

10 frankly speaking _____

11 not so much A as B _____

12 without regard to _____

13 be marked by _____

14 look up _____

15 regard A as B _____

16 back and forth _____

17 rule out _____

18 resort to _____

19 put on _____

20 so to speak _____

21 be endowed with _____

정답
01 ~가 있을 때에는
02 나란히
03 ~을 구성하다
04 ~을 제출하다
05 ~을 가능하게 하다
06 ~하는 데 익숙하다
07 ~하는 것이 낫다
08 ~을 멀리하다
09 과시하다
10 솔직히 말해서
11 A라기 보다는 오히려 B
12 ~에 상관없이
13 ~라는 특징을 갖다
14 ~을 찾다
15 A를 B로 여기다
16 앞뒤로
17 ~을 제외하다
18 ~에 의존하다
19 ~을 입다
20 말하자면
21 ~을 부여받다

Review Test

☑ 다음 숙어의 뜻을 우리말로 쓰시오.

01 rule out _____   12 be marked by _____

02 without regard to _____   13 back and forth _____

03 resort to _____   14 hand in _____

04 put on _____   15 show off _____

05 in the presence of _____   16 may as well V _____

06 frankly speaking _____   17 not so much A as B _____

07 regard A as B _____   18 so to speak _____

08 side by side _____   19 look up _____

09 allow for _____   20 be accustomed to 명사(-ing) _____

10 be endowed with _____   21 keep away from _____

11 make up _____

Review Test

☑️ 다음 숙어의 뜻을 우리말로 쓰시오.

01 not so much A as B _____

02 be accustomed to 명사(-ing) _____

03 keep away from _____

04 so to speak _____

05 look up _____

06 put on _____

07 resort to _____

08 allow for _____

09 back and forth _____

10 in the presence of _____

11 frankly speaking _____

12 make up _____

13 without regard to _____

14 be marked by _____

15 may as well V _____

16 rule out _____

17 be endowed with _____

18 hand in _____

19 regard A as B _____

20 side by side _____

21 show off _____

정답
01 A라기 보다는 오히려 B
02 ~하는 데 익숙하다
03 ~을 멀리하다
04 말하자면
05 ~을 찾다
06 ~을 입다
07 ~에 의존하다
08 ~을 가능하게 하다
09 앞뒤로
10 ~가 있을 때에는
11 솔직히 말해서
12 ~을 구성하다
13 ~에 상관없이
14 ~라는 특징을 갖다
15 ~하는 것이 낫다
16 ~을 제외하다
17 ~을 부여받다
18 ~을 제출하다
19 A를 B로 여기다
20 나란히
21 과시하다

295	
stand out	눈에 띄다

296	
by means of	~에 의하여

297	
place an order	주문하다

298	
stick to	~을 고수하다

299	
run after	~을 뒤쫓다

300	
center on	~을 중심으로 하다

301	
get back	~을 되찾다

302	
on a daily basis	매일

303	
take apart	~을 분해하다

304	
be anxious about	~을 걱정하다

305	
all of a sudden	갑자기

306	
at an angle	비스듬히

307	
be predicated on	~에 근거하다

308	
out of breath	숨이 차서

309	
by chance	우연히

310	
have no choice but to V	~하지 않을 수 없다

311	
apply to	~에게 적용되다

312	
the same goes for	~도 마찬가지이다

313	
be on the point of -ing	막 ~하려고 하다

314	
stop by	잠깐 들르다

315	
in general	일반적으로

Review Test

☑ 다음 숙어의 뜻을 우리말로 쓰시오.

01 out of breath ＿＿＿＿＿＿＿＿＿   12 by means of ＿＿＿＿＿＿＿＿＿

02 by chance ＿＿＿＿＿＿＿＿＿   13 place an order ＿＿＿＿＿＿＿＿＿

03 get back ＿＿＿＿＿＿＿＿＿   14 on a daily basis ＿＿＿＿＿＿＿＿＿

04 center on ＿＿＿＿＿＿＿＿＿   15 the same goes for ＿＿＿＿＿＿＿＿＿

05 at an angle ＿＿＿＿＿＿＿＿＿   16 in general ＿＿＿＿＿＿＿＿＿

06 take apart ＿＿＿＿＿＿＿＿＿   17 apply to ＿＿＿＿＿＿＿＿＿

07 all of a sudden ＿＿＿＿＿＿＿＿＿   18 have no choice but to V ＿＿＿＿＿＿＿＿＿

08 be predicated on ＿＿＿＿＿＿＿＿＿   19 run after ＿＿＿＿＿＿＿＿＿

09 be on the point of -ing ＿＿＿＿＿＿＿＿＿   20 stand out ＿＿＿＿＿＿＿＿＿

10 be anxious about ＿＿＿＿＿＿＿＿＿   21 stop by ＿＿＿＿＿＿＿＿＿

11 stick to ＿＿＿＿＿＿＿＿＿

정답	01 숨이 차서	10 ~을 걱정하다	19 ~을 뒤쫓다
	02 우연히	11 ~을 고수하다	20 눈에 띄다
	03 ~을 되찾다	12 ~에 의하여	21 잠깐 들르다
	04 ~을 중심으로 하다	13 주문하다	
	05 비스듬히	14 매일	
	06 ~을 분해하다	15 ~도 마찬가지이다	
	07 갑자기	16 일반적으로	
	08 ~에 근거하다	17 ~에게 적용되다	
	09 막 ~하려고 하다	18 ~하지 않을 수 없다	

Review Test

☑ 다음 숙어의 뜻을 우리말로 쓰시오.

01 run after _____

02 stick to _____

03 take apart _____

04 be anxious about _____

05 the same goes for _____

06 all of a sudden _____

07 be on the point of -ing _____

08 in general _____

09 by means of _____

10 at an angle _____

11 be predicated on _____

12 center on _____

13 get back _____

14 apply to _____

15 have no choice but to V _____

16 stand out _____

17 place an order _____

18 by chance _____

19 on a daily basis _____

20 out of breath _____

21 stop by _____

정답
01 ~을 뒤쫓다	10 비스듬히	19 매일
02 ~을 고수하다	11 ~에 근거하다	20 숨이 차서
03 ~을 분해하다	12 ~을 중심으로 하다	21 잠깐 들르다
04 ~을 걱정하다	13 ~을 되찾다	
05 ~도 마찬가지이다	14 ~에게 적용되다	
06 갑자기	15 ~하지 않을 수 없다	
07 막 ~하려고 하다	16 눈에 띄다	
08 일반적으로	17 주문하다	
09 ~에 의하여	18 우연히	

Review Test

☑ 다음 숙어의 뜻을 우리말로 쓰시오.

01 place an order _____

02 center on _____

03 by chance _____

04 on a daily basis _____

05 run after _____

06 at an angle _____

07 have no choice but to V _____

08 stick to _____

09 the same goes for _____

10 stop by _____

11 take apart _____

12 get back _____

13 stand out _____

14 be anxious about _____

15 by means of _____

16 be on the point of -ing _____

17 be predicated on _____

18 out of breath _____

19 apply to _____

20 all of a sudden _____

21 in general _____

정답

01 주문하다	10 잠깐 들르다	19 ~에게 적용되다
02 ~을 중심으로 하다	11 ~을 분해하다	20 갑자기
03 우연히	12 ~을 되찾다	21 일반적으로
04 매일	13 눈에 띄다	
05 ~을 뒤쫓다	14 ~을 걱정하다	
06 비스듬히	15 ~에 의하여	
07 ~하지 않을 수 없다	16 막 ~하려고 하다	
08 ~을 고수하다	17 ~에 근거하다	
09 ~도 마찬가지이다	18 숨이 차서	

316	
at first sight	언뜻 보기에

317	
have an effect on	~에 영향을 끼치다

318	
be made up of	~로 구성되다

319	
on duty	근무 중의

320	
be absorbed in	~에 열중하다

321	
thanks to	~때문에

322	
be characterized by	~라는 특징을 갖다

323	drop by	~에 잠깐 들르다
324	concentrate on	~에 집중하다
325	be good for	~에 유익하다
326	bring on	~을 초래하다
327	and so on	기타 등등
328	call on	~을 요구하다
329	have nothing to do with	~와 관계가 없다

330	on business	사업상
331	be anxious for	~을 갈망하다
332	in reality	사실상
333	leave no room for	~의 여지가 없다
334	at times	가끔
335	cannot ... too	아무리 ~해도 지나치지 않다
336	in no time	즉시

Review Test

☑ 다음 숙어의 뜻을 우리말로 쓰시오.

01 have nothing to do with _____   12 have an effect on _____

02 on business _____   13 be made up of _____

03 be characterized by _____   14 drop by _____

04 thanks to _____   15 leave no room for _____

05 and so on _____   16 in no time _____

06 concentrate on _____   17 in reality _____

07 bring on _____   18 be anxious for _____

08 call on _____   19 be absorbed in _____

09 at times _____   20 at first sight _____

10 be good for _____   21 cannot ... too _____

11 on duty _____

정답 | 01 ~와 관계가 없다 | 10 ~에 유익하다 | 19 ~에 열중하다
| 02 사업상 | 11 근무 중의 | 20 언뜻 보기에
| 03 ~라는 특징을 갖다 | 12 ~에 영향을 끼치다 | 21 아무리 ~해도 지나치지 않다
04 ~때문에	13 ~로 구성되다
05 기타 등등	14 ~에 잠깐 들르다
06 ~에 집중하다	15 ~의 여지가 없다
07 ~을 초래하다	16 즉시
08 ~을 요구하다	17 사실상
09 가끔	18 ~을 갈망하다

Review Test

☑ 다음 숙어의 뜻을 우리말로 쓰시오.

01 be absorbed in _____

02 on duty _____

03 concentrate on _____

04 be good for _____

05 leave no room for _____

06 bring on _____

07 at times _____

08 in no time _____

09 have an effect on _____

10 and so on _____

11 call on _____

12 thanks to _____

13 be characterized by _____

14 in reality _____

15 be anxious for _____

16 at first sight _____

17 be made up of _____

18 on business _____

19 drop by _____

20 have nothing to do with _____

21 cannot ... too _____

정답
01 ~에 열중하다
02 근무 중의
03 ~에 집중하다
04 ~에 유익하다
05 ~의 여지가 없다
06 ~을 초래하다
07 가끔
08 즉시
09 ~에 영향을 끼치다

10 기타 등등
11 ~을 요구하다
12 ~때문에
13 ~라는 특징을 갖다
14 사실상
15 ~을 갈망하다
16 언뜻 보기에
17 ~로 구성되다
18 사업상

19 ~에 잠깐 들르다
20 ~와 관계가 없다
21 아무리 ~해도 지나치지 않다

Review Test

☑ 다음 숙어의 뜻을 우리말로 쓰시오.

01 be made up of _____

02 thanks to _____

03 on business _____

04 drop by _____

05 be absorbed in _____

06 and so on _____

07 be anxious for _____

08 on duty _____

09 leave no room for _____

10 cannot ... too _____

11 concentrate on _____

12 be characterized by _____

13 at first sight _____

14 be good for _____

15 have an effect on _____

16 at times _____

17 call on _____

18 have nothing to do with _____

19 in reality _____

20 bring on _____

21 in no time _____

정답
01 ~로 구성되다
02 ~때문에
03 사업상
04 ~에 잠깐 들르다
05 ~에 열중하다
06 기타 등등
07 ~을 갈망하다
08 근무 중의
09 ~의 여지가 없다
10 아무리 ~해도 지나치지 않다
11 ~에 집중하다
12 ~라는 특징을 갖다
13 언뜻 보기에
14 ~에 유익하다
15 ~에 영향을 끼치다
16 가끔
17 ~을 요구하다
18 ~와 관계가 없다
19 사실상
20 ~을 초래하다
21 즉시

DAY 17 숙어

337
get across
이해시키다

338
bear in mind
명심하다

339
as a matter of fact
사실상

340
owing to
~때문에

341
sum up
~을 요약하다

342
be related to
~와 관련이 있다

343
in time
제시간에

344	to some extent	어느 정도
345	in person	직접
346	make an effort	노력하다
347	by the way	그런데
348	take notice of	~을 주목하다
349	in pairs	짝을 지어
350	more often than not	자주

351	
turn A into B	A를 B로 바꾸다

352	
get nowhere	아무 성과도 얻지 못하다

353	
used to V	~하곤 했다

354	
back up	~을 지지하다

355	
out of order	고장이 난

356	
a wide range of	매우 다양한

357	
account for	~을 설명하다

Review Test

☑️ 다음 숙어의 뜻을 우리말로 쓰시오.

01 in pairs _____   12 in person _____

02 by the way _____   13 be related to _____

03 account for _____   14 in time _____

04 more often than not _____   15 out of order _____

05 used to V _____   16 as a matter of fact _____

06 to some extent _____   17 a wide range of _____

07 turn A into B _____   18 make an effort _____

08 back up _____   19 get nowhere _____

09 get across _____   20 owing to _____

10 sum up _____   21 bear in mind _____

11 take notice of _____

정답
01 짝을 지어	10 ~을 요약하다	19 아무 성과도 얻지 못하다
02 그런데	11 ~을 주목하다	20 ~때문에
03 ~을 설명하다	12 직접	21 명심하다
04 자주	13 ~와 관련이 있다	
05 ~하곤 했다	14 제시간에	
06 어느 정도	15 고장이 난	
07 A를 B로 바꾸다	16 사실상	
08 ~을 지지하다	17 매우 다양한	
09 이해시키다	18 노력하다	

Review Test

☑ 다음 숙어의 뜻을 우리말로 쓰시오.

01 a wide range of _____

02 back up _____

03 make an effort _____

04 get across _____

05 be related to _____

06 to some extent _____

07 used to V _____

08 as a matter of fact _____

09 owing to _____

10 by the way _____

11 in person _____

12 get nowhere _____

13 take notice of _____

14 turn A into B _____

15 more often than not _____

16 bear in mind _____

17 account for _____

18 in time _____

19 out of order _____

20 sum up _____

21 in pairs _____

정답
01 매우 다양한
02 ~을 지지하다
03 노력하다
04 이해시키다
05 ~와 관련이 있다
06 어느 정도
07 ~하곤 했다
08 사실상
09 ~때문에

10 그런데
11 직접
12 아무 성과도 얻지 못하다
13 ~을 주목하다
14 A를 B로 바꾸다
15 자주
16 명심하다
17 ~을 설명하다
18 제시간에

19 고장이 난
20 ~을 요약하다
21 짝을 지어

Review Test

☑ 다음 숙어의 뜻을 우리말로 쓰시오.

01 sum up _____   12 as a matter of fact _____

02 to some extent _____   13 get across _____

03 owing to _____   14 in time _____

04 more often than not _____   15 account for _____

05 make an effort _____   16 out of order _____

06 get nowhere _____   17 by the way _____

07 in pairs _____   18 bear in mind _____

08 used to V _____   19 in person _____

09 back up _____   20 take notice of _____

10 be related to _____   21 a wide range of _____

11 turn A into B _____

정답   01 ~을 요약하다   10 ~와 관련이 있다   19 직접
       02 어느 정도   11 A를 B로 바꾸다   20 ~을 주목하다
       03 ~때문에   12 사실상   21 매우 다양한
       04 자주   13 이해시키다
       05 노력하다   14 제시간에
       06 아무 성과도 얻지 못하다   15 ~을 설명하다
       07 짝을 지어   16 고장이 난
       08 ~하곤 했다   17 그런데
       09 ~을 지지하다   18 명심하다

103

358	
all at once	갑자기

359	
stem from	~에서 생겨나다

360	
It is no use ~ing	~해도 소용없다

361	
at the expense of	~을 희생하여

362	
from now on	지금부터

363	
do away with	~을 없애다

364	
as far as	~하는 한

365		
keep A from B		A가 B하는 것을 막다

366		
come to an end		끝나다

367		
get stuck in		~에 갇히다

368		
be equipped with		~을 갖추고 있다

369		
stand in line		줄을 서다

370		
look back on		회상하다

371		
make a reservation		예약하다

372 at hand	가까이에 있는
373 be followed by	다음에 ~가 이어지다
374 cope with	~에 대처하다
375 toss and turn	몸을 뒤척이다
376 in charge of	~을 맡고 있는
377 settle down	정착하다
378 cut in line	새치기하다

Review Test

☑ 다음 숙어의 뜻을 우리말로 쓰시오.

01 come to an end		12 It is no use ~ing	
02 be followed by		13 be equipped with	
03 toss and turn		14 do away with	
04 make a reservation		15 keep A from B	
05 get stuck in		16 settle down	
06 as far as		17 stem from	
07 at hand		18 in charge of	
08 cut in line		19 cope with	
09 from now on		20 stand in line	
10 all at once		21 at the expense of	
11 look back on			

정답
01 끝나다	10 갑자기	19 ~에 대처하다
02 다음에 ~가 이어지다	11 회상하다	20 줄을 서다
03 몸을 뒤척이다	12 ~해도 소용없다	21 ~을 희생하여
04 예약하다	13 ~을 갖추고 있다	
05 ~에 갇히다	14 ~을 없애다	
06 ~하는 한	15 A가 B하는 것을 막다	
07 가까이에 있는	16 정착하다	
08 새치기하다	17 ~에서 생겨나다	
09 지금부터	18 ~을 맡고 있는	

Review Test

☑ 다음 숙어의 뜻을 우리말로 쓰시오.

01 cut in line _____

02 cope with _____

03 as far as _____

04 make a reservation _____

05 at the expense of _____

06 all at once _____

07 settle down _____

08 in charge of _____

09 get stuck in _____

10 come to an end _____

11 keep A from B _____

12 at hand _____

13 be equipped with _____

14 look back on _____

15 from now on _____

16 do away with _____

17 stem from _____

18 be followed by _____

19 It is no use ~ing _____

20 toss and turn _____

21 stand in line _____

정답

01 새치기하다	10 끝나다	19 ~해도 소용없다
02 ~에 대처하다	11 A가 B하는 것을 막다	20 몸을 뒤척이다
03 ~하는 한	12 가까이에 있는	21 줄을 서다
04 예약하다	13 ~을 갖추고 있다	
05 ~을 희생하여	14 회상하다	
06 갑자기	15 지금부터	
07 정착하다	16 ~을 없애다	
08 ~을 맡고 있는	17 ~에서 생겨나다	
09 ~에 갇히다	18 다음에 ~가 이어지다	

Review Test

☑ 다음 숙어의 뜻을 우리말로 쓰시오.

01 make a reservation	_____	12 keep A from B	_____
02 all at once	_____	13 cut in line	_____
03 get stuck in	_____	14 come to an end	_____
04 be followed by	_____	15 cope with	_____
05 as far as	_____	16 be equipped with	_____
06 look back on	_____	17 do away with	_____
07 stem from	_____	18 at the expense of	_____
08 from now on	_____	19 It is no use ~ing	_____
09 in charge of	_____	20 settle down	_____
10 at hand	_____	21 toss and turn	_____
11 stand in line	_____		

정답
01 예약하다
02 갑자기
03 ~에 갇히다
04 다음에 ~가 이어지다
05 ~하는 한
06 회상하다
07 ~에서 생겨나다
08 지금부터
09 ~을 맡고 있는

10 가까이에 있는
11 줄을 서다
12 A가 B하는 것을 막다
13 새치기하다
14 끝나다
15 ~에 대처하다
16 ~을 갖추고 있다
17 ~을 없애다
18 ~을 희생하여

19 ~해도 소용없다
20 정착하다
21 몸을 뒤척이다

379	
take a day off	하루 휴가를 내다

380	
after a while	잠시 후

381	
force A to B	A에게 강제로 B하게 하다

382	
hold good	유효하다

383	
correspond to (with)	~와 일치하다

384	
in need	어려움에 처한

385	
fill in	기입하다

386	might as well V	~하는 것이 낫다
387	in abundance	많이
388	at one's disposal	~의 마음대로
389	in line with	~와 일치하는
390	in depth	자세히
391	in particular	특히
392	leave out	~을 생략하다

393	
in itself	그 자체로

394	
take pains	노력하다

395	
by the same token	같은 이유로

396	
there is no -ing	~하는 것은 불가능하다

397	
up to	~까지

398	
scores of	수십의

399	
along with	~와 함께

Review Test

☑ 다음 숙어의 뜻을 우리말로 쓰시오.

01 might as well V		12 up to	
02 leave out		13 along with	
03 there is no -ing		14 correspond to (with)	
04 in abundance		15 scores of	
05 hold good		16 take a day off	
06 in particular		17 force A to B	
07 in itself		18 by the same token	
08 in need		19 take pains	
09 fill in		20 after a while	
10 in depth		21 in line with	
11 at one's disposal			

정답

01 ~하는 것이 낫다
02 ~을 생략하다
03 ~하는 것은 불가능하다
04 많이
05 유효하다
06 특히
07 그 자체로
08 어려움에 처한
09 기입하다
10 자세히
11 ~의 마음대로
12 ~까지
13 ~와 함께
14 ~와 일치하다
15 수십의
16 하루 휴가를 내다
17 A에게 강제로 B하게 하다
18 같은 이유로
19 노력하다
20 잠시 후
21 ~와 일치하는

113

Review Test

☑ 다음 숙어의 뜻을 우리말로 쓰시오.

01 in abundance _____

02 take pains _____

03 after a while _____

04 force A to B _____

05 scores of _____

06 take a day off _____

07 fill in _____

08 hold good _____

09 in line with _____

10 leave out _____

11 in particular _____

12 along with _____

13 in itself _____

14 might as well V _____

15 there is no -ing _____

16 in depth _____

17 in need _____

18 at one's disposal _____

19 correspond to (with) _____

20 by the same token _____

21 up to _____

정답
01 많이
02 노력하다
03 잠시 후
04 A에게 강제로 B하게 하다
05 수십의
06 하루 휴가를 내다
07 기입하다
08 유효하다
09 ~와 일치하는
10 ~을 생략하다
11 특히
12 ~와 함께
13 그 자체로
14 ~하는 것이 낫다
15 ~하는 것은 불가능하다
16 자세히
17 어려움에 처한
18 ~의 마음대로
19 ~와 일치하다
20 같은 이유로
21 ~까지

Review Test

☑ 다음 숙어의 뜻을 우리말로 쓰시오.

01 in line with _____   12 force A to B _____

02 along with _____   13 there is no -ing _____

03 by the same token _____   14 at one's disposal _____

04 fill in _____   15 in itself _____

05 up to _____   16 hold good _____

06 after a while _____   17 take a day off _____

07 in particular _____   18 in depth _____

08 in need _____   19 leave out _____

09 in abundance _____   20 scores of _____

10 correspond to (with) _____ 21 take pains _____

11 might as well V _____

정답   01 ~와 일치하는   10 ~와 일치하다   19 ~을 생략하다
       02 ~와 함께   11 ~하는 것이 낫다   20 수십의
       03 같은 이유로   12 A에게 강제로 B하게 하다 21 노력하다
       04 기입하다   13 ~하는 것은 불가능하다
       05 ~까지   14 ~의 마음대로
       06 잠시 후   15 그 자체로
       07 특히   16 유효하다
       08 어려움에 처한   17 하루 휴가를 내다
       09 많이   18 자세히

400	
except for	~을 제외하고

401	
never fail to V	반드시 ~하다

402	
let go of	~을 놓아주다

403	
hit on	생각나다

404	
what is more	게다가

405	
on a regular basis	정기적으로

406	
break out	발생하다

407	
carry out	~을 수행하다

408	
be tired of	~에 싫증이 나다

409	
get A to B	A가 B하게 하다

410	
get to V	~하게 되다

411	
give birth to	~을 낳다

412	
fill up	채우다

413	
at the sight of	~을 보고는

414	
confuse A with B	A와 B를 혼동하다

415	
at length	자세히

416	
be accompanied by	~을 동반하다

417	
be faced with	~에 직면하다

418	
take turns	교대로 하다

419	
furnish A with B	A에게 B를 공급하다

420	
in the long run	결국

Review Test

☑ 다음 숙어의 뜻을 우리말로 쓰시오.

01 be accompanied by	12 confuse A with B
02 on a regular basis	13 at length
03 furnish A with B	14 fill up
04 be tired of	15 except for
05 be faced with	16 carry out
06 break out	17 never fail to V
07 in the long run	18 get to V
08 get A to B	19 hit on
09 at the sight of	20 take turns
10 give birth to	21 let go of
11 what is more	

정답 01 ~을 동반하다   10 ~을 낳다   19 생각나다
      02 정기적으로   11 게다가   20 교대로 하다
      03 A에게 B를 공급하다   12 A와 B를 혼동하다   21 ~을 놓아주다
      04 ~에 싫증이 나다   13 자세히
      05 ~에 직면하다   14 채우다
      06 발생하다   15 ~을 제외하고
      07 결국   16 ~을 수행하다
      08 A가 B하게 하다   17 반드시 ~하다
      09 ~을 보고는   18 ~하게 되다

Review Test

☑ 다음 숙어의 뜻을 우리말로 쓰시오.

01 hit on _____   12 get to V _____

02 on a regular basis _____   13 fill up _____

03 be accompanied by _____   14 at length _____

04 in the long run _____   15 let go of _____

05 except for _____   16 confuse A with B _____

06 furnish A with B _____   17 take turns _____

07 at the sight of _____   18 get A to B _____

08 carry out _____   19 never fail to V _____

09 be tired of _____   20 give birth to _____

10 be faced with _____   21 what is more _____

11 break out _____

정답   01 생각나다   10 ~에 직면하다   19 반드시 ~하다
       02 정기적으로   11 발생하다   20 ~을 낳다
       03 ~을 동반하다   12 ~하게 되다   21 게다가
       04 결국   13 채우다
       05 ~을 제외하고   14 자세히
       06 A에게 B를 공급하다   15 ~을 놓아주다
       07 ~을 보고는   16 A와 B를 혼동하다
       08 ~을 수행하다   17 교대로 하다
       09 ~에 실증이 나다   18 A가 B하게 하다

Review Test

☑ 다음 숙어의 뜻을 우리말로 쓰시오.

01	give birth to	_____	12	on a regular basis	_____
02	be accompanied by	_____	13	hit on	_____
03	take turns	_____	14	at length	_____
04	at the sight of	_____	15	furnish A with B	_____
05	confuse A with B	_____	16	be tired of	_____
06	fill up	_____	17	let go of	_____
07	never fail to V	_____	18	be faced with	_____
08	in the long run	_____	19	except for	_____
09	get A to B	_____	20	what is more	_____
10	carry out	_____	21	break out	_____
11	get to V	_____			

정답

01 ~을 낳다	10 ~을 수행하다	19 ~을 제외하고
02 ~을 동반하다	11 ~하게 되다	20 게다가
03 교대로 하다	12 정기적으로	21 발생하다
04 ~을 보고는	13 생각나다	
05 A와 B를 혼동하다	14 자세히	
06 채우다	15 A에게 B를 공급하다	
07 반드시 ~하다	16 ~에 싫증이 나다	
08 결국	17 ~을 놓아주다	
09 A가 B하게 하다	18 ~에 직면하다	

421	
all the way	줄곧

422	
call for	~을 요구하다

423	
a multitude of	많은

424	
take place	발생하다

425	
cause A to B	A가 B하게 하다

426	
kind of	다소

427	
not more than	기껏해야

428	for good	영원히

429	get rid of	~을 제거하다

430	star in	~에 주연을 맡다

431	pay off	성과를 올리다

432	other than	~이외의

433	have in mind	~을 염두에 두다

434	take measures	조치를 취하다

435	
get into	~에 들어가다

436	
sooner or later	조만간

437	
remind A of B	A에게 B가 생각나게 하다

438	
blame A for B	B에 대해 A를 비난하다

439	
a couple of	두셋의

440	
such A as B	B와 같은 A

441	
break through	~을 극복하다

Review Test

☑ 다음 숙어의 뜻을 우리말로 쓰시오.

01 have in mind _____

02 get into _____

03 remind A of B _____

04 call for _____

05 blame A for B _____

06 other than _____

07 pay off _____

08 take measures _____

09 a couple of _____

10 cause A to B _____

11 all the way _____

12 sooner or later _____

13 get rid of _____

14 kind of _____

15 break through _____

16 a multitude of _____

17 for good _____

18 take place _____

19 star in _____

20 not more than _____

21 such A as B _____

정답
01 ~을 염두에 두다
02 ~에 들어가다
03 A에게 B가 생각나게 하다
04 ~을 요구하다
05 B에 대해 A를 비난하다
06 ~이외의
07 성과를 올리다
08 조치를 취하다
09 두셋의

10 A가 B하게 하다
11 줄곧
12 조만간
13 ~을 제거하다
14 다소
15 ~을 극복하다
16 많은
17 영원히
18 발생하다

19 ~에 주연을 맡다
20 기껏해야
21 B와 같은 A

125

Review Test

☑ 다음 숙어의 뜻을 우리말로 쓰시오.

01 break through _____ 12 call for _____

02 such A as B _____ 13 a couple of _____

03 cause A to B _____ 14 kind of _____

04 blame A for B _____ 15 a multitude of _____

05 star in _____ 16 other than _____

06 have in mind _____ 17 remind A of B _____

07 get into _____ 18 get rid of _____

08 all the way _____ 19 take place _____

09 for good _____ 20 pay off _____

10 not more than _____ 21 sooner or later _____

11 take measures _____

정답 01 ~을 극복하다   10 기껏해야   19 발생하다
      02 B와 같은 A   11 조치를 취하다   20 성과를 올리다
      03 A가 B하게 하다   12 ~을 요구하다   21 조만간
      04 B에 대해 A를 비난하다   13 두셋의
      05 ~에 주연을 맡다   14 다소
      06 ~을 염두에 두다   15 많은
      07 ~에 들어가다   16 ~이외의
      08 줄곧   17 A에게 B가 생각나게 하다
      09 영원히   18 ~을 제거하다

Review Test

☑ 다음 숙어의 뜻을 우리말로 쓰시오.

01 a multitude of _____

02 other than _____

03 sooner or later _____

04 blame A for B _____

05 a couple of _____

06 kind of _____

07 get into _____

08 take place _____

09 not more than _____

10 for good _____

11 have in mind _____

12 cause A to B _____

13 break through _____

14 all the way _____

15 remind A of B _____

16 take measures _____

17 pay off _____

18 star in _____

19 call for _____

20 such A as B _____

21 get rid of _____

정답 01 많은
      02 ~이외의
      03 조만간
      04 B에 대해 A를 비난하다
      05 두셋의
      06 다소
      07 ~에 들어가다
      08 발생하다
      09 기껏해야
      10 영원히
      11 ~을 염두에 두다
      12 A가 B하게 하다
      13 ~을 극복하다
      14 줄곧
      15 A에게 B가 생각나게 하다
      16 조치를 취하다
      17 성과를 올리다
      18 ~에 주연을 맡다
      19 ~을 요구하다
      20 B와 같은 A
      21 ~을 제거하다

442	as for	~에 관하여
443	as a whole	대체로
444	be covered with	~로 덮여 있다
445	have no idea	전혀 모르다
446	in the absence of	~이 없을 때에
447	first of all	무엇보다
448	get through	~을 헤쳐 나가다

449	make up one's mind	마음을 정하다
450	contribute to	~의 원인이 되다
451	be apt to V	~하기 쉽다
452	take care of	~을 돌보다
453	on the air	방송 중인
454	fall back on	~에 의존하다
455	out of fashion	유행이 지난

456 be relevant to	~와 관련이 있다
457 simply put	간단히 말해서
458 for nothing	공짜로
459 hand down	~을 물려주다
460 put ~ into action	~을 실행에 옮기다
461 result in	~의 결과를 가져오다
462 go through	~을 경험하다

Review Test

☑ 다음 숙어의 뜻을 우리말로 쓰시오.

01 in the absence of _____   12 have no idea _____

02 for nothing _____   13 contribute to _____

03 out of fashion _____   14 fall back on _____

04 result in _____   15 hand down _____

05 as for _____   16 as a whole _____

06 make up one's mind _____   17 get through _____

07 be covered with _____   18 simply put _____

08 put ~ into action _____   19 go through _____

09 be relevant to _____   20 be apt to V _____

10 on the air _____   21 take care of _____

11 first of all _____

정답   01 ~이 없을 때에   10 방송 중인   19 ~을 경험하다
      02 공짜로   11 무엇보다   20 ~하기 쉽다
      03 유행이 지난   12 전혀 모르다   21 ~을 돌보다
      04 ~의 결과를 가져오다   13 ~의 원인이 되다
      05 ~에 관하여   14 ~에 의존하다
      06 마음을 정하다   15 ~을 물려주다
      07 ~로 덮여 있다   16 대체로
      08 ~을 실행에 옮기다   17 ~을 헤쳐 나가다
      09 ~와 관련이 있다   18 간단히 말해서

131

Review Test ───────

☑ 다음 숙어의 뜻을 우리말로 쓰시오.

01 on the air _____

02 simply put _____

03 be relevant to _____

04 for nothing _____

05 fall back on _____

06 as a whole _____

07 contribute to _____

08 put ~ into action _____

09 out of fashion _____

10 first of all _____

11 hand down _____

12 take care of _____

13 be covered with _____

14 make up one's mind _____

15 get through _____

16 result in _____

17 be apt to V _____

18 in the absence of _____

19 go through _____

20 have no idea _____

21 as for _____

정답
01 방송 중인
02 간단히 말해서
03 ~와 관련이 있다
04 공짜로
05 ~에 의존하다
06 대체로
07 ~의 원인이 되다
08 ~을 실행에 옮기다
09 유행이 지난

10 무엇보다
11 ~을 물려주다
12 ~을 돌보다
13 ~로 덮여 있다
14 마음을 정하다
15 ~을 헤쳐 나가다
16 ~의 결과를 가져오다
17 ~하기 쉽다
18 ~이 없을 때에

19 ~을 경험하다
20 전혀 모르다
21 ~에 관하여

Review Test

☑ 다음 숙어의 뜻을 우리말로 쓰시오.

01 for nothing _____

02 result in _____

03 in the absence of _____

04 as a whole _____

05 have no idea _____

06 simply put _____

07 fall back on _____

08 be covered with _____

09 be apt to V _____

10 be relevant to _____

11 contribute to _____

12 put ~ into action _____

13 on the air _____

14 take care of _____

15 as for _____

16 go through _____

17 first of all _____

18 out of fashion _____

19 hand down _____

20 make up one's mind _____

21 get through _____

정답
01 공짜로
02 ~의 결과를 가져오다
03 ~이 없을 때에
04 대체로
05 전혀 모르다
06 간단히 말해서
07 ~에 의존하다
08 ~로 덮여 있다
09 ~하기 쉽다

10 ~와 관련이 있다
11 ~의 원인이 되다
12 ~을 실행에 옮기다
13 방송 중인
14 ~을 돌보다
15 ~에 관하여
16 ~을 경험하다
17 무엇보다
18 유행이 지난

19 ~을 물려주다
20 마음을 정하다
21 ~을 헤쳐 나가다

463	
vote against	반대표를 던지다

464	
as of	~시점에

465	
get in the way	방해가 되다

466	
before long	머지않아

467	
wake up	깨다

468	
give away	~을 나누어 주다

469	
from time to time	가끔

470		
so far		지금까지

471		
pick out		~을 고르다

472		
separate A from B		A를 B에서 분리하다

473		
behind the wheel		운전하는

474		
be possessed with		~에 사로잡혀 있다

475		
at all times		항상

476		
compare A to B		A와 B를 비교하다

477		
to tell the truth		사실대로 말하자면

478		
on sale		판매 중인

479		
in conclusion		결론적으로

480		
between ourselves		우리끼리 이야기지만

481		
keep pace with		~와 보조를 맞추다

482		
ask for		~을 요청하다

483		
be used to 명사(-ing)		~에 익숙하다

☑ 다음 숙어의 뜻을 우리말로 쓰시오.

01 in conclusion _____

02 on sale _____

03 separate A from B _____

04 get in the way _____

05 ask for _____

06 at all times _____

07 give away _____

08 be possessed with _____

09 be used to 명사(-ing) _____

10 to tell the truth _____

11 from time to time _____

12 behind the wheel _____

13 pick out _____

14 as of _____

15 vote against _____

16 compare A to B _____

17 between ourselves _____

18 before long _____

19 keep pace with _____

20 wake up _____

21 so far _____

정답

01 결론적으로
02 판매 중인
03 A를 B에서 분리하다
04 방해가 되다
05 ~을 요청하다
06 항상
07 ~을 나누어 주다
08 ~에 사로잡혀 있다
09 ~에 익숙하다

10 사실대로 말하자면
11 가끔
12 운전하는
13 ~을 고르다
14 ~시점에
15 반대표를 던지다
16 A와 B를 비교하다
17 우리끼리 이야기지만
18 머지않아

19 ~와 보조를 맞추다
20 깨다
21 지금까지

Review Test

01 get in the way _____   12 on sale _____

02 so far _____   13 to tell the truth _____

03 give away _____   14 separate A from B _____

04 wake up _____   15 ask for _____

05 compare A to B _____   16 between ourselves _____

06 keep pace with _____   17 as of _____

07 before long _____   18 vote against _____

08 in conclusion _____   19 be used to 명사(-ing) _____

09 from time to time _____   20 at all times _____

10 behind the wheel _____   21 pick out _____

11 be possessed with _____

정답
01 방해가 되다	10 운전하는	19 ~에 익숙하다
02 지금까지	11 ~에 사로잡혀 있다	20 항상
03 ~을 나누어 주다	12 판매 중인	21 ~을 고르다
04 깨다	13 사실대로 말하자면	
05 A와 B를 비교하다	14 A를 B에서 분리하다	
06 ~와 보조를 맞추다	15 ~을 요청하다	
07 머지않아	16 우리끼리 이야기지만	
08 결론적으로	17 ~시점에	
09 가끔	18 반대표를 던지다	

Review Test

☑ 다음 숙어의 뜻을 우리말로 쓰시오.

01 compare A to B _____   12 as of _____

02 to tell the truth _____   13 get in the way _____

03 from time to time _____   14 so far _____

04 give away _____   15 between ourselves _____

05 be possessed with _____   16 be used to 명사(-ing) _____

06 pick out _____   17 in conclusion _____

07 behind the wheel _____   18 on sale _____

08 at all times _____   19 wake up _____

09 keep pace with _____   20 vote against _____

10 separate A from B _____   21 ask for _____

11 before long _____

정답
01 A와 B를 비교하다	10 A를 B에서 분리하다	19 깨다
02 사실대로 말하자면	11 머지않아	20 반대표를 던지다
03 가끔	12 ~시점에	21 ~을 요청하다
04 ~을 나누어 주다	13 방해가 되다	
05 ~에 사로잡혀 있다	14 지금까지	
06 ~을 고르다	15 우리끼리 이야기지만	
07 운전하는	16 ~에 익숙하다	
08 항상	17 결론적으로	
09 ~와 보조를 맞추다	18 판매 중인	

139

DAY 24　숙어

484		
amount to		합계가 ~에 달하다

485		
weed out		~을 제거하다

486		
in honor of		~을 기념하여

487		
devoid of		~이 없는

488		
put away		~을 치우다

489		
dispose of		~을 처분하다

490		
stick around		가지 않고 있다

491 do harm	해가 되다
492 quite a little	꽤 많은
493 in a row	연속으로
494 look down on	~을 경멸하다
495 change A into B	A를 B로 바꾸다
496 make a suggestion	제안하다
497 see A as B	A를 B로 여기다

498	apart from	~은 제외하고
499	cling to	~에 매달리다
500	go so far as to V	~까지도 하다
501	off duty	근무시간 외인
502	~ as well	~도 또한
503	major in	~을 전공하다
504	keep off	~을 차단하다

Review Test

☑ 다음 숙어의 뜻을 우리말로 쓰시오.

01 put away   12 dispose of

02 devoid of   13 stick around

03 quite a little   14 go so far as to V

04 in a row   15 cling to

05 off duty   16 amount to

06 look down on   17 in honor of

07 ~ as well   18 apart from

08 keep off   19 do harm

09 weed out   20 see A as B

10 change A into B   21 major in

11 make a suggestion

정답

01 ~을 치우다	10 A를 B로 바꾸다	19 해가 되다
02 ~이 없는	11 제안하다	20 A를 B로 여기다
03 꽤 많은	12 ~을 처분하다	21 ~을 전공하다
04 연속으로	13 가지 않고 있다	
05 근무시간 외인	14 ~까지도 하다	
06 ~을 경멸하다	15 ~에 매달리다	
07 ~도 또한	16 합계가 ~에 달하다	
08 ~을 차단하다	17 ~을 기념하여	
09 ~을 제거하다	18 ~은 제외하고	

Review Test ────────────

☑ 다음 숙어의 뜻을 우리말로 쓰시오.

01 in honor of _____

02 dispose of _____

03 apart from _____

04 do harm _____

05 put away _____

06 change A into B _____

07 cling to _____

08 devoid of _____

09 off duty _____

10 major in _____

11 quite a little _____

12 stick around _____

13 amount to _____

14 in a row _____

15 weed out _____

16 ~ as well _____

17 make a suggestion _____

18 see A as B _____

19 go so far as to V _____

20 look down on _____

21 keep off _____

정답
01 ~을 기념하여
02 ~을 처분하다
03 ~은 제외하고
04 해가 되다
05 ~을 치우다
06 A를 B로 바꾸다
07 ~에 매달리다
08 ~이 없는
09 근무시간 외인

10 ~을 전공하다
11 꽤 많은
12 가지 않고 있다
13 합계가 ~에 달하다
14 연속으로
15 ~을 제거하다
16 ~도 또한
17 제안하다
18 A를 B로 여기다

19 ~까지도 하다
20 ~을 경멸하다
21 ~을 차단하다

Review Test

☑ 다음 숙어의 뜻을 우리말로 쓰시오.

01 make a suggestion _____

02 look down on _____

03 keep off _____

04 see A as B _____

05 go so far as to V _____

06 do harm _____

07 apart from _____

08 off duty _____

09 amount to _____

10 put away _____

11 change A into B _____

12 quite a little _____

13 dispose of _____

14 stick around _____

15 ~ as well _____

16 in honor of _____

17 major in _____

18 in a row _____

19 cling to _____

20 devoid of _____

21 weed out _____

정답
01 제안하다
02 ~을 경멸하다
03 ~을 차단하다
04 A를 B로 여기다
05 ~까지도 하다
06 해가 되다
07 ~은 제외하고
08 근무시간 외인
09 합계가 ~에 달하다

10 ~을 치우다
11 A를 B로 바꾸다
12 꽤 많은
13 ~을 처분하다
14 가지 않고 있다
15 ~도 또한
16 ~을 기념하여
17 ~을 전공하다
18 연속으로

19 ~에 매달리다
20 ~이 없는
21 ~을 제거하다

505	in accord with	~와 일치하여
506	hand over	~을 건네주다
507	take ~ into account	~을 고려하다
508	as a consequence	그 결과
509	under construction	건축 중인
510	look after	~을 돌보다
511	lose sight of	~을 놓치다

512	
on a large scale	대규모로

513	
depend on	~에 의존하다

514	
work through	~을 해결하다

515	
by any chance	혹시라도

516	
run out of	다 써 버리다

517	
nothing more than	~일 뿐인

518	
reach for	~로 손을 뻗다

#	표현	뜻
519	at any cost	어떻게 해서라도
520	out of stock	품절된
521	break into	~에 침입하다
522	make it	성공하다
523	here and there	여기저기
524	happen to V	우연히 ~하다
525	be caught up in	~에 휘말리다

☑ 다음 숙어의 뜻을 우리말로 쓰시오.

01 happen to V	_____	12 out of stock	_____
02 make it	_____	13 run out of	_____
03 work through	_____	14 at any cost	_____
04 in accord with	_____	15 reach for	_____
05 look after	_____	16 hand over	_____
06 on a large scale	_____	17 be caught up in	_____
07 break into	_____	18 lose sight of	_____
08 take ~ into account	_____	19 here and there	_____
09 as a consequence	_____	20 under construction	_____
10 by any chance	_____	21 nothing more than	_____
11 depend on	_____		

정답

01 우연히 ~하다	10 혹시라도	19 여기저기
02 성공하다	11 ~에 의존하다	20 건축 중인
03 ~을 해결하다	12 품절된	21 ~일 뿐인
04 ~와 일치하여	13 다 써 버리다	
05 ~을 돌보다	14 어떻게 해서라도	
06 대규모로	15 ~로 손을 뻗다	
07 ~에 침입하다	16 ~을 건네주다	
08 ~을 고려하다	17 ~에 휘말리다	
09 그 결과	18 ~을 놓치다	

Review Test

☑ 다음 숙어의 뜻을 우리말로 쓰시오.

01 under construction

02 on a large scale

03 as a consequence

04 reach for

05 work through

06 out of stock

07 nothing more than

08 break into

09 make it

10 look after

11 at any cost

12 take ~ into account

13 in accord with

14 lose sight of

15 be caught up in

16 here and there

17 by any chance

18 hand over

19 depend on

20 run out of

21 happen to V

정답   01 건축 중인   10 ~을 돌보다   19 ~에 의존하다
      02 대규모로   11 어떻게 해서라도   20 다 써 버리다
      03 그 결과   12 ~을 고려하다   21 우연히 ~하다
      04 ~로 손을 뻗다   13 ~와 일치하여
      05 ~을 해결하다   14 ~을 놓치다
      06 품절된   15 ~에 휘말리다
      07 ~일 뿐인   16 여기저기
      08 ~에 침입하다   17 혹시라도
      09 성공하다   18 ~을 건네주다

Review Test

☑ 다음 숙어의 뜻을 우리말로 쓰시오.

01 depend on		12 take ~ into account
02 out of stock		13 by any chance
03 make it		14 look after
04 reach for		15 on a large scale
05 work through		16 happen to V
06 lose sight of		17 hand over
07 at any cost		18 here and there
08 be caught up in		19 break into
09 under construction		20 run out of
10 in accord with		21 as a consequence
11 nothing more than		

정답
01 ~에 의존하다	10 ~와 일치하여	19 ~에 침입하다
02 품절된	11 ~일 뿐인	20 다 써 버리다
03 성공하다	12 ~을 고려하다	21 그 결과
04 ~로 손을 뻗다	13 혹시라도	
05 ~을 해결하다	14 ~을 돌보다	
06 ~을 놓치다	15 대규모로	
07 어떻게 해서라도	16 우연히 ~하다	
08 ~에 휘말리다	17 ~을 건네주다	
09 건축 중인	18 여기저기	

DAY 26 숙어

526	
neither A nor B	A와 B 둘 다 ~아니다

527	
a variety of	다양한

528	
enable A to B	A가 B할 수 있게 하다

529	
out of sight	안 보이는

530	
distinguish A from B	A와 B를 구별하다

531	
be short of	~이 부족하다

532	
in that	~라는 점에서

533	given that	~을 고려하면
534	keep an eye on	~을 감시하다
535	be charged with	~이 맡겨지다
536	lead to	~을 이끌어 내다
537	give rise to	~을 일으키다
538	in practice	실제로
539	come up with	~을 생각해 내다

540	
in no way	결코 ~ 않다

541	
be involved in	~에 참가하다

542	
run into	~을 우연히 만나다

543	
be unaware of	~을 모르고 있다

544	
clear A of B	A로부터 B를 제거하다

545	
come about	~가 생기다

546	
let alone	~은 말할 것도 없고

Review Test

☑ 다음 숙어의 뜻을 우리말로 쓰시오.

01 let alone _____

02 run into _____

03 in that _____

04 come up with _____

05 out of sight _____

06 neither A nor B _____

07 come about _____

08 clear A of B _____

09 be charged with _____

10 keep an eye on _____

11 given that _____

12 in no way _____

13 lead to _____

14 in practice _____

15 distinguish A from B _____

16 be short of _____

17 a variety of _____

18 be involved in _____

19 enable A to B _____

20 be unaware of _____

21 give rise to _____

정답
01 ~은 말할 것도 없고	10 ~을 감시하다	19 A가 B할 수 있게 하다
02 ~을 우연히 만나다	11 ~을 고려하면	20 ~을 모르고 있다
03 ~라는 점에서	12 결코 ~ 않다	21 ~을 일으키다
04 ~을 생각해 내다	13 ~을 이끌어 내다	
05 안 보이는	14 실제로	
06 A와 B 둘 다 ~아니다	15 A와 B를 구별하다	
07 ~가 생기다	16 ~이 부족하다	
08 A로부터 B를 제거하다	17 다양한	
09 ~이 맡겨지다	18 ~에 참가하다	

Review Test

☑ 다음 숙어의 뜻을 우리말로 쓰시오.

01 come up with _____ 12 given that _____

02 neither A nor B _____ 13 let alone _____

03 be charged with _____ 14 keep an eye on _____

04 be involved in _____ 15 run into _____

05 in that _____ 16 lead to _____

06 in practice _____ 17 be short of _____

07 a variety of _____ 18 out of sight _____

08 distinguish A from B _____ 19 enable A to B _____

09 clear A of B _____ 20 come about _____

10 in no way _____ 21 be unaware of _____

11 give rise to _____

정답
01 ~을 생각해 내다
02 A와 B 둘 다 ~아니다
03 ~이 맡겨지다
04 ~에 참가하다
05 ~라는 점에서
06 실제로
07 다양한
08 A와 B를 구별하다
09 A로부터 B를 제거하다

10 결코 ~ 않다
11 ~을 일으키다
12 ~을 고려하면
13 ~은 말할 것도 없고
14 ~을 감시하다
15 ~을 우연히 만나다
16 ~을 이끌어 내다
17 ~이 부족하다
18 안 보이는

19 A가 B할 수 있게 하다
20 ~가 생기다
21 ~을 모르고 있다

Review Test

☑️ **다음 숙어의 뜻을 우리말로 쓰시오.**

01 given that _____

02 come up with _____

03 be unaware of _____

04 keep an eye on _____

05 out of sight _____

06 in practice _____

07 in no way _____

08 be short of _____

09 in that _____

10 give rise to _____

11 be charged with _____

12 clear A of B _____

13 let alone _____

14 distinguish A from B _____

15 lead to _____

16 neither A nor B _____

17 enable A to B _____

18 run into _____

19 be involved in _____

20 a variety of _____

21 come about _____

정답
01 ~을 고려하면
02 ~을 생각해 내다
03 ~을 모르고 있다
04 ~을 감시하다
05 안 보이는
06 실제로
07 결코 ~ 않다
08 ~이 부족하다
09 ~라는 점에서

10 ~을 일으키다
11 ~이 맡겨지다
12 A로부터 B를 제거하다
13 ~은 말할 것도 없고
14 A와 B를 구별하다
15 ~을 이끌어 내다
16 A와 B 둘 다 ~아니다
17 A가 B할 수 있게 하다
18 ~을 우연히 만나다

19 ~에 참가하다
20 다양한
21 ~가 생기다

547
miss out on
~을 놓치다

548
tap into
~을 이용하다

549
take on
~을 떠맡다

550
make sense
의미가 통하다

551
If it were not for
만일 ~가 없다면

552
up to date
최신의

553
from side to side
좌우로

554	
in advance	미리

555	
run away	도망가다

556	
care for	~을 돌보다

557	
at work	작용하는

558	
without question	의심할 여지없이

559	
take after	~을 닮다

560	
once upon a time	옛날에

561	work out	~을 해결하다

562	and the like	기타 등등

563	most of all	무엇보다도

564	keep track of	~을 추적하다

565	based on	~에 근거하여

566	take advantage of	~을 이용하다

567	as is often the case with	~에 흔히 있는 일이지만

Review Test

☑ 다음 숙어의 뜻을 우리말로 쓰시오.

01 run away _____   12 as is often the case with _____

02 and the like _____   13 work out _____

03 tap into _____   14 in advance _____

04 take on _____   15 keep track of _____

05 take advantage of _____   16 without question _____

06 miss out on _____   17 up to date _____

07 from side to side _____   18 care for _____

08 make sense _____   19 If it were not for _____

09 at work _____   20 most of all _____

10 once upon a time _____   21 based on _____

11 take after _____

정답			
01 도망가다	10 옛날에	19 만일 ~가 없다면	
02 기타 등등	11 ~을 닮다	20 무엇보다도	
03 ~을 이용하다	12 ~에 흔히 있는 일이지만	21 ~에 근거하여	
04 ~을 떠맡다	13 ~을 해결하다		
05 ~을 이용하다	14 미리		
06 ~을 놓치다	15 ~을 추적하다		
07 좌우로	16 의심할 여지없이		
08 의미가 통하다	17 최신의		
09 작용하는	18 ~을 돌보다		

Review Test

☑ 다음 숙어의 뜻을 우리말로 쓰시오.

01 once upon a time _____

02 work out _____

03 from side to side _____

04 up to date _____

05 without question _____

06 run away _____

07 at work _____

08 take after _____

09 based on _____

10 care for _____

11 make sense _____

12 tap into _____

13 take on _____

14 in advance _____

15 keep track of _____

16 as is often the case with _____

17 most of all _____

18 and the like _____

19 If it were not for _____

20 miss out on _____

21 take advantage of _____

정답
01 옛날에
02 ~을 해결하다
03 좌우로
04 최신의
05 의심할 여지없이
06 도망가다
07 작용하는
08 ~을 닮다
09 ~에 근거하여
10 ~을 돌보다
11 의미가 통하다
12 ~을 이용하다
13 ~을 떠맡다
14 미리
15 ~을 추적하다
16 ~에 흔히 있는 일이지만
17 무엇보다도
18 기타 등등
19 만일 ~가 없다면
20 ~을 놓치다
21 ~을 이용하다

☑ 다음 숙어의 뜻을 우리말로 쓰시오.

01 If it were not for _____

02 make sense _____

03 run away _____

04 care for _____

05 keep track of _____

06 at work _____

07 based on _____

08 as is often the case with _____

09 tap into _____

10 without question _____

11 take after _____

12 up to date _____

13 from side to side _____

14 most of all _____

15 and the like _____

16 miss out on _____

17 take on _____

18 work out _____

19 in advance _____

20 once upon a time _____

21 take advantage of _____

정답
01 만일 ~가 없다면
02 의미가 통하다
03 도망가다
04 ~을 돌보다
05 ~을 추적하다
06 작용하는
07 ~에 근거하여
08 ~에 흔히 있는 일이지만
09 ~을 이용하다

10 의심할 여지없이
11 ~을 닮다
12 최신의
13 좌우로
14 무엇보다도
15 기타 등등
16 ~을 놓치다
17 ~을 떠맡다
18 ~을 해결하다

19 미리
20 옛날에
21 ~을 이용하다

568	
out of control	통제할 수 없는

569	
a range of	다양한

570	
warm up	준비 운동을 하다

571	
in brief	간단히 말해서

572	
in response to	~에 대한 반응으로

573	
come through	해내다

574	
be suspicious of	~을 의심하다

575	
what we call	이른바

576	
in spite of	~에도 불구하고

577	
on the verge of	곧 ~할 것 같은

578	
lay out	~을 배치하다

579	
strictly speaking	엄밀하게 말해서

580	
in stock	재고가 남아 있는

581	
in view of	~의 관점에서 볼 때

582	
be obsessed with	~에 집착하다

583	
owe A to B	A는 B의 덕택이다

584	
in distinction to	~와 구별하여

585	
keep up with	~을 따라가다

586	
at first glance	언뜻 보기에

587	
at best	기껏해야

588	
participate in	~에 참여하다

Review Test

☑️ 다음 숙어의 뜻을 우리말로 쓰시오.

01 in response to _____   12 in brief _____

02 come through _____   13 in spite of _____

03 on the verge of _____   14 keep up with _____

04 what we call _____   15 warm up _____

05 in stock _____   16 lay out _____

06 in distinction to _____   17 participate in _____

07 be obsessed with _____   18 owe A to B _____

08 at best _____   19 out of control _____

09 at first glance _____   20 in view of _____

10 strictly speaking _____   21 be suspicious of _____

11 a range of _____

정답
01 ~에 대한 반응으로	10 엄밀하게 말해서	19 통제할 수 없는
02 해내다	11 다양한	20 ~의 관점에서 볼 때
03 곧 ~할 것 같은	12 간단히 말해서	21 ~을 의심하다
04 이른바	13 ~에도 불구하고	
05 재고가 남아 있는	14 ~을 따라가다	
06 ~와 구별하여	15 준비 운동을 하다	
07 ~에 집착하다	16 ~을 배치하다	
08 기껏해야	17 ~에 참여하다	
09 언뜻 보기에	18 A는 B의 덕택이다	

Review Test

☑️ 다음 숙어의 뜻을 우리말로 쓰시오.

01 warm up _____   12 be suspicious of _____

02 come through _____   13 out of control _____

03 be obsessed with _____   14 on the verge of _____

04 what we call _____   15 a range of _____

05 in response to _____   16 at first glance _____

06 strictly speaking _____   17 in stock _____

07 owe A to B _____   18 in view of _____

08 in brief _____   19 in distinction to _____

09 keep up with _____   20 lay out _____

10 at best _____   21 participate in _____

11 in spite of _____

정답
01 준비 운동을 하다
02 해내다
03 ~에 집착하다
04 이른바
05 ~에 대한 반응으로
06 엄밀하게 말해서
07 A는 B의 덕택이다
08 간단히 말해서
09 ~을 따라가다

10 기껏해야
11 ~에도 불구하고
12 ~을 의심하다
13 통제할 수 없는
14 곧 ~할 것 같은
15 다양한
16 언뜻 보기에
17 재고가 남아 있는
18 ~의 관점에서 볼 때

19 ~와 구별하여
20 ~을 배치하다
21 ~에 참여하다

Review Test

☑ **다음 숙어의 뜻을 우리말로 쓰시오.**

01 in stock _____

02 lay out _____

03 participate in _____

04 in view of _____

05 in distinction to _____

06 what we call _____

07 be obsessed with _____

08 keep up with _____

09 out of control _____

10 in response to _____

11 strictly speaking _____

12 in spite of _____

13 come through _____

14 be suspicious of _____

15 at first glance _____

16 warm up _____

17 at best _____

18 on the verge of _____

19 owe A to B _____

20 in brief _____

21 a range of _____

정답

01 재고가 남아 있는
02 ~을 배치하다
03 ~에 참여하다
04 ~의 관점에서 볼 때
05 ~와 구별하여
06 이른바
07 ~에 집착하다
08 ~을 따라가다
09 통제할 수 없는

10 ~에 대한 반응으로
11 엄밀하게 말해서
12 ~에도 불구하고
13 해내다
14 ~을 의심하다
15 언뜻 보기에
16 준비 운동을 하다
17 기껏해야
18 곧 ~할 것 같은

19 A는 B의 덕택이다
20 간단히 말해서
21 다양한

169

589	
out of tune	조화되지 않는

590	
sign up for	~을 신청하다

591	
feel like -ing	~을 하고 싶다

592	
dress up	잘 차려입다

593	
set ~ apart from ...	~을 ...와 구별하다

594	
bring A to B	A를 B로 가져오다

595	
be obliged to	~하지 않을 수 없다

596	be responsible for	~의 원인이 되다
597	in harmony with	~와 조화롭게
598	be determined to V	~하기로 결심하다
599	set out	출발하다
600	put ~ together	~을 구성하다
601	be poor at	~을 잘하지 못하다
602	by no means	결코 ~ 아닌

603 be predisposed to V	~하는 경향이 있다
604 a host of	많은
605 in accordance with	~와 일치하여
606 be tied to	~와 관련이 있다
607 ascribe A to B	A를 B의 탓이라고 하다
608 as follows	다음과 같이
609 refer to A as B	A를 B라고 부르다

Review Test

☑ 다음 숙어의 뜻을 우리말로 쓰시오.

01 as follows _____

02 be tied to _____

03 be determined to V _____

04 out of tune _____

05 bring A to B _____

06 be responsible for _____

07 in accordance with _____

08 feel like -ing _____

09 dress up _____

10 set out _____

11 in harmony with _____

12 a host of _____

13 put ~ together _____

14 be predisposed to V _____

15 by no means _____

16 sign up for _____

17 refer to A as B _____

18 be obliged to _____

19 ascribe A to B _____

20 set ~ apart from ... _____

21 be poor at _____

정답

01 다음과 같이
02 ~와 관련이 있다
03 ~하기로 결심하다
04 조화되지 않는
05 A를 B로 가져오다
06 ~의 원인이 되다
07 ~와 일치하여
08 ~을 하고 싶다
09 잘 차려입다

10 출발하다
11 ~와 조화롭게
12 많은
13 ~을 구성하다
14 ~하는 경향이 있다
15 결코 ~ 아닌
16 ~을 신청하다
17 A를 B라고 부르다
18 ~하지 않을 수 없다

19 A를 B의 탓이라고 하다
20 ~을 ...와 구별하다
21 ~을 잘하지 못하다

Review Test ━━━━━━━━━━━━━━━━━━━━

☑ 다음 숙어의 뜻을 우리말로 쓰시오.

01 by no means _____

02 be predisposed to V _____

03 be obliged to _____

04 bring A to B _____

05 put ~ together _____

06 in harmony with _____

07 set out _____

08 be poor at _____

09 ascribe A to B _____

10 be determined to V _____

11 dress up _____

12 sign up for _____

13 feel like -ing _____

14 be responsible for _____

15 be tied to _____

16 refer to A as B _____

17 in accordance with _____

18 a host of _____

19 set ~ apart from ... _____

20 out of tune _____

21 as follows _____

정답

01 결코 ~ 아닌
02 ~하는 경향이 있다
03 ~하지 않을 수 없다
04 A를 B로 가져오다
05 ~을 구성하다
06 ~와 조화롭게
07 출발하다
08 ~을 잘하지 못하다
09 A를 B의 탓이라고 하다

10 ~하기로 결심하다
11 잘 차려입다
12 ~을 신청하다
13 ~을 하고 싶다
14 ~의 원인이 되다
15 ~와 관련이 있다
16 A를 B라고 부르다
17 ~와 일치하여
18 많은

19 ~을 ...와 구별하다
20 조화되지 않는
21 다음과 같이

Review Test

☑ **다음 숙어의 뜻을 우리말로 쓰시오.**

01 set ~ apart from ...

02 dress up

03 in harmony with

04 be determined to V

05 be tied to

06 set out

07 ascribe A to B

08 refer to A as B

09 sign up for

10 put ~ together

11 be poor at

12 bring A to B

13 be obliged to

14 in accordance with

15 a host of

16 out of tune

17 feel like -ing

18 be predisposed to V

19 be responsible for

20 by no means

21 as follows

정답			
	01 ~을 ...와 구별하다	10 ~을 구성하다	19 ~의 원인이 되다
	02 잘 차려입다	11 ~을 잘하지 못하다	20 결코 ~ 아닌
	03 ~와 조화롭게	12 A를 B로 가져오다	21 다음과 같이
	04 ~하기로 결심하다	13 ~하지 않을 수 없다	
	05 ~와 관련이 있다	14 ~와 일치하여	
	06 출발하다	15 많은	
	07 A를 B의 탓이라고 하다	16 조화되지 않는	
	08 A를 B라고 부르다	17 ~을 하고 싶다	
	09 ~을 신청하다	18 ~하는 경향이 있다	

175

DAY 30　숙어

| 610 | with a view to | ~할 목적으로 |

| 611 | take steps | 조치를 취하다 |

| 612 | be superior to | ~보다 우월하다 |

| 613 | a number of | 많은 |

| 614 | step in | 개입하다 |

| 615 | in any case | 어쨌든 |

| 616 | day after day | 날마다 |

617	
carry on	~을 계속하다

618	
divide A into B	A를 B로 나누다

619	
be prone to	~하기 쉽다

620	
nothing but	~일 뿐인

621	
pass out	~을 나눠 주다

622	
more than	~이상

623	
get on	~을 타다

624	
be equated with	~와 동일시되다

625	
lose track of	~을 놓치다

626	
set free	~을 놓아주다

627	
enter into	~을 시작하다

628	
to the contrary	그와 반대되는

629	
be true of	~에게 해당되다

630	
take A for B	A를 B라고 생각하다

Review Test

☑ 다음 숙어의 뜻을 우리말로 쓰시오.

01 step in _____   12 a number of _____

02 in any case _____   13 divide A into B _____

03 be prone to _____   14 enter into _____

04 carry on _____   15 be superior to _____

05 more than _____   16 nothing but _____

06 set free _____   17 take A for B _____

07 be equated with _____   18 lose track of _____

08 be true of _____   19 with a view to _____

09 to the contrary _____   20 get on _____

10 pass out _____   21 day after day _____

11 take steps _____

정답
01 개입하다	10 ~을 나눠 주다	19 ~할 목적으로
02 어쨌든	11 조치를 취하다	20 ~을 타다
03 ~하기 쉽다	12 많은	21 날마다
04 ~을 계속하다	13 A를 B로 나누다	
05 ~이상	14 ~을 시작하다	
06 ~을 놓아주다	15 ~보다 우월하다	
07 ~와 동일시되다	16 ~일 뿐인	
08 ~에게 해당되다	17 A를 B라고 생각하다	
09 그와 반대되는	18 ~을 놓치다	

Review Test ────────────

☑ 다음 숙어의 뜻을 우리말로 쓰시오.

01 be superior to _____

02 in any case _____

03 be equated with _____

04 carry on _____

05 step in _____

06 pass out _____

07 lose track of _____

08 a number of _____

09 enter into _____

10 be true of _____

11 divide A into B _____

12 day after day _____

13 with a view to _____

14 be prone to _____

15 take steps _____

16 to the contrary _____

17 more than _____

18 get on _____

19 set free _____

20 nothing but _____

21 take A for B _____

정답
01 ~보다 우월하다
02 어쨌든
03 ~와 동일시되다
04 ~을 계속하다
05 개입하다
06 ~을 나눠 주다
07 ~을 놓치다
08 많은
09 ~을 시작하다

10 ~에게 해당되다
11 A를 B로 나누다
12 날마다
13 ~할 목적으로
14 ~하기 쉽다
15 조치를 취하다
16 그와 반대되는
17 ~이상
18 ~을 타다

19 ~을 놓아주다
20 ~일 뿐인
21 A를 B라고 생각하다

Review Test

☑ 다음 숙어의 뜻을 우리말로 쓰시오.

01 more than _____

02 nothing but _____

03 take A for B _____

04 get on _____

05 set free _____

06 carry on _____

07 be equated with _____

08 enter into _____

09 with a view to _____

10 step in _____

11 pass out _____

12 divide A into B _____

13 in any case _____

14 day after day _____

15 to the contrary _____

16 be superior to _____

17 be true of _____

18 be prone to _____

19 lose track of _____

20 a number of _____

21 take steps _____

정답
01 ~이상	10 개입하다	19 ~을 놓치다
02 ~일 뿐인	11 ~을 나눠 주다	20 많은
03 A를 B라고 생각하다	12 A를 B로 나누다	21 조치를 취하다
04 ~을 타다	13 어쨌든	
05 ~을 놓아주다	14 날마다	
06 ~을 계속하다	15 그와 반대되는	
07 ~와 동일시되다	16 ~보다 우월하다	
08 ~을 시작하다	17 ~에게 해당되다	
09 ~할 목적으로	18 ~하기 쉽다	

181

631
in favor of
~을 찬성하여

632
come true
실현되다

633
as it were
말하자면

634
plenty of
많은

635
all but
~을 제외하고는 모두

636
tell A from B
A와 B를 구별하다

637
set about
~을 시작하다

638	object to 명사(-ing)	~에 반대하다
639	be subject to	~의 영향을 받다
640	point to	~을 가리키다
641	be crowded with	~로 붐비다
642	come near -ing	하마터면 ~할 뻔하다
643	one another	서로
644	in the long term	장기적으로

645	
on one's part	~의 편에서는

646	
for free	무료로

647	
pass down	~을 전해주다

648	
to a large extent	대부분

649	
look through	~을 훑어보다

650	
count on	~에 의존하다

651	
refrain from -ing	~하는 것을 삼가다

Review Test

☑ 다음 숙어의 뜻을 우리말로 쓰시오.

01 count on _____

02 to a large extent _____

03 point to _____

04 in favor of _____

05 tell A from B _____

06 object to 명사(-ing) _____

07 pass down _____

08 as it were _____

09 plenty of _____

10 be crowded with _____

11 be subject to _____

12 for free _____

13 come near -ing _____

14 on one's part _____

15 in the long term _____

16 come true _____

17 refrain from -ing _____

18 set about _____

19 look through _____

20 all but _____

21 one another _____

정답
01 ~에 의존하다	10 ~로 붐비다
02 대부분	11 ~의 영향을 받다
03 ~을 가리키다	12 무료로
04 ~을 찬성하여	13 하마터면 ~할 뻔하다
05 A와 B를 구별하다	14 ~의 편에서는
06 ~에 반대하다	15 장기적으로
07 ~을 전해주다	16 실현되다
08 말하자면	17 ~하는 것을 삼가다
09 많은	18 ~을 시작하다

19 ~을 훑어보다
20 ~을 제외하고는 모두
21 서로

Review Test

☑ 다음 숙어의 뜻을 우리말로 쓰시오.

01 all but _____

02 object to 명사(-ing) _____

03 plenty of _____

04 in the long term _____

05 point to _____

06 for free _____

07 one another _____

08 pass down _____

09 to a large extent _____

10 tell A from B _____

11 on one's part _____

12 as it were _____

13 in favor of _____

14 set about _____

15 refrain from -ing _____

16 look through _____

17 be crowded with _____

18 come true _____

19 be subject to _____

20 come near -ing _____

21 count on _____

정답   01 ~을 제외하고는 모두   10 A와 B를 구별하다   19 ~의 영향을 받다
       02 ~에 반대하다   11 ~의 편에서는   20 하마터면 ~할 뻔하다
       03 많은   12 말하자면   21 ~에 의존하다
       04 장기적으로   13 ~을 찬성하여
       05 ~을 가리키다   14 ~을 시작하다
       06 무료로   15 ~하는 것을 삼가다
       07 서로   16 ~을 훑어보다
       08 ~을 전해주다   17 ~로 붐비다
       09 대부분   18 실현되다

Review Test

☑ 다음 숙어의 뜻을 우리말로 쓰시오.

01 be subject to _____   12 as it were _____

02 for free _____   13 be crowded with _____

03 to a large extent _____   14 tell A from B _____

04 in the long term _____   15 object to 명사(-ing) _____

05 point to _____   16 count on _____

06 set about _____   17 come true _____

07 on one's part _____   18 look through _____

08 refrain from -ing _____   19 pass down _____

09 all but _____   20 come near -ing _____

10 in favor of _____   21 plenty of _____

11 one another _____

정답
01 ~의 영향을 받다   10 ~을 찬성하여   19 ~을 전해주다
02 무료로   11 서로   20 하마터면 ~할 뻔하다
03 대부분   12 말하자면   21 많은
04 장기적으로   13 ~로 붐비다
05 ~을 가리키다   14 A와 B를 구별하다
06 ~을 시작하다   15 ~에 반대하다
07 ~의 편에서는   16 ~에 의존하다
08 ~하는 것을 삼가다   17 실현되다
09 ~을 제외하고는 모두   18 ~을 훑어보다

652
turn into

~로 변하다

- - - - - - - - - - - - - - - - - - -

653
go against

~을 반대하다

- - - - - - - - - - - - - - - - - - -

654
kick off

~을 시작하다

- - - - - - - - - - - - - - - - - - -

655
turn out

입증되다

- - - - - - - - - - - - - - - - - - -

656
go after

뒤쫓다

- - - - - - - - - - - - - - - - - - -

657
on the contrary

그와는 반대로

- - - - - - - - - - - - - - - - - - -

658
be into

~에 관심이 많다

- - - - - - - - - - - - - - - - - - -

659	take off	~을 벗다
660	out of date	구식의
661	cannot but V	~하지 않을 수 없다
662	such and such	이러저러한
663	take over	~을 떠맡다
664	be free from	~이 없다
665	A as well as B	B뿐만 아니라 A 또한

666	
serve as	~으로 역할을 하다

667	
set ~ free	~을 풀어 주다

668	
one after another	차례로

669	
in pursuit of	~을 추구하여

670	
rob A of B	A로부터 B를 빼앗다

671	
an array of	많은

672	
pull over	차를 세우다

Review Test

☑️ 다음 숙어의 뜻을 우리말로 쓰시오.

01 pull over _____

02 one after another _____

03 be into _____

04 A as well as B _____

05 turn out _____

06 turn into _____

07 an array of _____

08 rob A of B _____

09 cannot but V _____

10 out of date _____

11 take off _____

12 serve as _____

13 such and such _____

14 be free from _____

15 go after _____

16 on the contrary _____

17 go against _____

18 set ~ free _____

19 kick off _____

20 in pursuit of _____

21 take over _____

정답
01 차를 세우다
02 차례로
03 ~에 관심이 많다
04 B뿐만 아니라 A 또한
05 입증되다
06 ~로 변하다
07 많은
08 A로부터 B를 빼앗다
09 ~하지 않을 수 없다

10 구식의
11 ~을 벗다
12 ~으로 역할을 하다
13 이러저러한
14 ~이 없다
15 뒤쫓다
16 그와는 반대로
17 ~을 반대하다
18 ~을 풀어 주다

19 ~을 시작하다
20 ~을 추구하여
21 ~을 떠맡다

Review Test

☑️ 다음 숙어의 뜻을 우리말로 쓰시오.

01 A as well as B   12 take off

02 turn into   13 pull over

03 cannot but V   14 out of date

04 set ~ free   15 one after another

05 be into   16 such and such

06 be free from   17 on the contrary

07 go against   18 turn out

08 go after   19 kick off

09 rob A of B   20 an array of

10 serve as   21 in pursuit of

11 take over

정답
01 B뿐만 아니라 A 또한	10 ~으로 역할을 하다	19 ~을 시작하다
02 ~로 변하다	11 ~을 떠맡다	20 많은
03 ~하지 않을 수 없다	12 ~을 벗다	21 ~을 추구하여
04 ~을 풀어 주다	13 차를 세우다	
05 ~에 관심이 많다	14 구식의	
06 ~이 없다	15 차례로	
07 ~을 반대하다	16 이러저러한	
08 뒤쫓다	17 그와는 반대로	
09 A로부터 B를 빼앗다	18 입증되다	

Review Test

☑ 다음 숙어의 뜻을 우리말로 쓰시오.

01 take off _____	12 rob A of B _____
02 A as well as B _____	13 pull over _____
03 in pursuit of _____	14 go after _____
04 out of date _____	15 such and such _____
05 turn out _____	16 turn into _____
06 be free from _____	17 kick off _____
07 serve as _____	18 one after another _____
08 on the contrary _____	19 set ~ free _____
09 be into _____	20 go against _____
10 take over _____	21 an array of _____
11 cannot but V _____	

정답

01 ~을 벗다	10 ~을 떠맡다	19 ~을 풀어 주다
02 B뿐만 아니라 A 또한	11 ~하지 않을 수 없다	20 ~을 반대하다
03 ~을 추구하여	12 A로부터 B를 빼앗다	21 많은
04 구식의	13 차를 세우다	
05 입증되다	14 뒤쫓다	
06 ~이 없다	15 이러저러한	
07 ~으로 역할을 하다	16 ~로 변하다	
08 그와는 반대로	17 ~을 시작하다	
09 ~에 관심이 많다	18 차례로	

DAY 33 숙어

673 apply for ~에 지원하다

674 at once 즉시

675 never ~ but ... ~하면 반드시 ...하다

676 check out ~을 확인하다

677 at least 적어도

678 in any event 어쨌든

679 fall short of ~에 미치지 못하다

680	
out of place	제자리에 있지 않은

681	
turn in	~을 제출하다

682	
relate to	~와 관련이 있다

683	
give off	~을 방출하다

684	
on the rise	증가하고 있는

685	
out of nowhere	갑자기

686	
convert A into B	A를 B로 바꾸다

687	
head for	~로 향하다

688	
from all walks of life	각계각층의

689	
stand by	대기하다

690	
lie in	~에 있다

691	
mean to V	~을 의도하다

692	
so long as	~하는 한

693	
convince A of B	A에게 B를 납득시키다

Review Test

☑ 다음 숙어의 뜻을 우리말로 쓰시오.

01 turn in _____

02 from all walks of life _____

03 at once _____

04 never ~ but ... _____

05 so long as _____

06 apply for _____

07 fall short of _____

08 check out _____

09 give off _____

10 convert A into B _____

11 out of nowhere _____

12 convince A of B _____

13 head for _____

14 out of place _____

15 lie in _____

16 on the rise _____

17 in any event _____

18 relate to _____

19 at least _____

20 stand by _____

21 mean to V _____

정답
01 ~을 제출하다
02 각계각층의
03 즉시
04 ~하면 반드시 ...하다
05 ~하는 한
06 ~에 지원하다
07 ~에 미치지 못하다
08 ~을 확인하다
09 ~을 방출하다

10 A를 B로 바꾸다
11 갑자기
12 A에게 B를 납득시키다
13 ~로 향하다
14 제자리에 있지 않은
15 ~에 있다
16 증가하고 있는
17 어쨌든
18 ~와 관련이 있다

19 적어도
20 대기하다
21 ~을 의도하다

Review Test

☑ 다음 숙어의 뜻을 우리말로 쓰시오.

01 give off _____   12 never ~ but ... _____

02 convince A of B _____   13 lie in _____

03 stand by _____   14 relate to _____

04 fall short of _____   15 head for _____

05 mean to V _____   16 check out _____

06 at once _____   17 apply for _____

07 out of nowhere _____   18 on the rise _____

08 in any event _____   19 convert A into B _____

09 turn in _____   20 so long as _____

10 at least _____   21 from all walks of life _____

11 out of place _____

정답
01 ~을 방출하다	10 적어도	19 A를 B로 바꾸다
02 A에게 B를 납득시키다	11 제자리에 있지 않은	20 ~하는 한
03 대기하다	12 ~하면 반드시 ...하다	21 각계각층의
04 ~에 미치지 못하다	13 ~에 있다	
05 ~을 의도하다	14 ~와 관련이 있다	
06 즉시	15 ~로 향하다	
07 갑자기	16 ~을 확인하다	
08 어쨌든	17 ~에 지원하다	
09 ~을 제출하다	18 증가하고 있는	

198

Review Test

☑ 다음 숙어의 뜻을 우리말로 쓰시오.

01 stand by ＿＿＿＿＿＿＿

02 in any event ＿＿＿＿＿＿＿

03 so long as ＿＿＿＿＿＿＿

04 turn in ＿＿＿＿＿＿＿

05 lie in ＿＿＿＿＿＿＿

06 fall short of ＿＿＿＿＿＿＿

07 convince A of B ＿＿＿＿＿＿＿

08 relate to ＿＿＿＿＿＿＿

09 convert A into B ＿＿＿＿＿＿＿

10 on the rise ＿＿＿＿＿＿＿

11 at least ＿＿＿＿＿＿＿

12 head for ＿＿＿＿＿＿＿

13 from all walks of life ＿＿＿＿＿＿＿

14 out of nowhere ＿＿＿＿＿＿＿

15 apply for ＿＿＿＿＿＿＿

16 out of place ＿＿＿＿＿＿＿

17 at once ＿＿＿＿＿＿＿

18 give off ＿＿＿＿＿＿＿

19 check out ＿＿＿＿＿＿＿

20 mean to V ＿＿＿＿＿＿＿

21 never ~ but ... ＿＿＿＿＿＿＿

정답
01 대기하다
02 어쨌든
03 ~하는 한
04 ~을 제출하다
05 ~에 있다
06 ~에 미치지 못하다
07 A에게 B를 납득시키다
08 ~와 관련이 있다
09 A를 B로 바꾸다

10 증가하고 있는
11 적어도
12 ~로 향하다
13 각계각층의
14 갑자기
15 ~에 지원하다
16 제자리에 있지 않은
17 즉시
18 ~을 방출하다

19 ~을 확인하다
20 ~을 의도하다
21 ~하면 반드시 ...하다

DAY 34 숙어

694
right away
즉시

695
needless to say
말할 필요도 없이

696
rest on
~에 의존하다

697
to make matters worse
설상가상으로

698
upside down
거꾸로

699
consist of
~로 구성되다

700
in the midst of
~의 한가운데

701 behind the times	시대에 뒤떨어진
702 take part in	~에 참여하다
703 in proportion to	~에 비례하여
704 get off	~에서 내리다
705 keep a promise	약속을 지키다
706 look for	~을 찾다
707 come to V	~하게 되다

708	what is worse	설상가상으로
709	point out	~을 지적하다
710	no less than	~에 못지않게
711	for a while	잠시 동안
712	by all means	반드시
713	pass on	~을 넘겨주다
714	fill A with B	A를 B로 채우다

☑ 다음 숙어의 뜻을 우리말로 쓰시오.

01 to make matters worse   12 get off

02 consist of   13 look for

03 no less than   14 point out

04 fill A with B   15 rest on

05 right away   16 what is worse

06 pass on   17 by all means

07 come to V   18 in proportion to

08 behind the times   19 needless to say

09 take part in   20 keep a promise

10 for a while   21 upside down

11 in the midst of

정답			
	01 설상가상으로	10 잠시 동안	19 말할 필요도 없이
	02 ~로 구성되다	11 ~의 한가운데	20 약속을 지키다
	03 ~에 못지않게	12 ~에서 내리다	21 거꾸로
	04 A를 B로 채우다	13 ~을 찾다	
	05 즉시	14 ~을 지적하다	
	06 ~을 넘겨주다	15 ~에 의존하다	
	07 ~하게 되다	16 설상가상으로	
	08 시대에 뒤떨어진	17 반드시	
	09 ~에 참여하다	18 ~에 비례하여	

Review Test

☑ 다음 숙어의 뜻을 우리말로 쓰시오.

01 come to V _____   12 needless to say _____

02 what is worse _____   13 rest on _____

03 in the midst of _____ 14 behind the times _____

04 consist of _____   15 for a while _____

05 keep a promise _____ 16 fill A with B _____

06 take part in _____   17 no less than _____

07 get off _____   18 point out _____

08 look for _____   19 upside down _____

09 by all means _____   20 right away _____

10 in proportion to _____ 21 pass on _____

11 to make matters worse _____

정답
01 ~하게 되다
02 설상가상으로
03 ~의 한가운데
04 ~로 구성되다
05 약속을 지키다
06 ~에 참여하다
07 ~에서 내리다
08 ~을 찾다
09 반드시

10 ~에 비례하여
11 설상가상으로
12 말할 필요도 없이
13 ~에 의존하다
14 시대에 뒤떨어진
15 잠시 동안
16 A를 B로 채우다
17 ~에 못지않게
18 ~을 지적하다

19 거꾸로
20 즉시
21 ~을 넘겨주다

Review Test

☑ 다음 숙어의 뜻을 우리말로 쓰시오.

01 upside down	_____	12 consist of	_____
02 to make matters worse	_____	13 in the midst of	_____
03 take part in	_____	14 no less than	_____
04 in proportion to	_____	15 point out	_____
05 for a while	_____	16 right away	_____
06 get off	_____	17 rest on	_____
07 by all means	_____	18 what is worse	_____
08 fill A with B	_____	19 behind the times	_____
09 needless to say	_____	20 come to V	_____
10 keep a promise	_____	21 pass on	_____
11 look for	_____		

정답

01 거꾸로	10 약속을 지키다	19 시대에 뒤떨어진
02 설상가상으로	11 ~을 찾다	20 ~하게 되다
03 ~에 참여하다	12 ~로 구성되다	21 ~을 넘겨주다
04 ~에 비례하여	13 ~의 한가운데	
05 잠시 동안	14 ~에 못지않게	
06 ~에서 내리다	15 ~을 지적하다	
07 반드시	16 즉시	
08 A를 B로 채우다	17 ~에 의존하다	
09 말할 필요도 없이	18 설상가상으로	

715	
be over	끝나다

716	
not only A but (also) B	A뿐만 아니라 B 또한

717	
range from A to B	A에서 B까지 걸쳐 있다

718	
inquire into	~을 조사하다

719	
fade away	사라지다

720	
have an influence on	~에 영향을 미치다

721	
put together	~을 조립하다

722	for the time being	당분간
723	be acquainted with	~을 알고 있다
724	be fond of	~을 좋아하다
725	be expected to V	~라고 예상되다
726	stop A from B(-ing)	A가 B하는 것을 막다
727	look over	~을 검토하다
728	bring together	~을 합치다

729	
as to	~에 관하여

730	
in short	간단히 말하면

731	
get lost	길을 잃다

732	
be dependent on	~에 의존하다

733	
the other day	며칠 전에

734	
show up	나타나다

735	
put out	불을 끄다

Review Test

☑️ 다음 숙어의 뜻을 우리말로 쓰시오.

01 fade away	_____	12 inquire into	_____
02 have an influence on	_____	13 be acquainted with	_____
03 be fond of	_____	14 be dependent on	_____
04 for the time being	_____	15 range from A to B	_____
05 look over	_____	16 be expected to V	_____
06 get lost	_____	17 put out	_____
07 as to	_____	18 in short	_____
08 show up	_____	19 be over	_____
09 the other day	_____	20 bring together	_____
10 stop A from B(-ing)	_____	21 put together	_____
11 not only A but (also) B	_____		

정답

01 사라지다
02 ~에 영향을 미치다
03 ~을 좋아하다
04 당분간
05 ~을 검토하다
06 길을 잃다
07 ~에 관하여
08 나타나다
09 며칠 전에

10 A가 B하는 것을 막다
11 A뿐만 아니라 B 또한
12 ~을 조사하다
13 ~을 알고 있다
14 ~에 의존하다
15 A에서 B까지 걸쳐 있다
16 ~라고 예상되다
17 불을 끄다
18 간단히 말하면

19 끝나다
20 ~을 합치다
21 ~을 조립하다

Review Test

☑ 다음 숙어의 뜻을 우리말로 쓰시오.

01 range from A to B

02 have an influence on

03 as to

04 for the time being

05 fade away

06 stop A from B(-ing)

07 in short

08 inquire into

09 be dependent on

10 show up

11 be acquainted with

12 put together

13 be over

14 be fond of

15 not only A but (also) B

16 the other day

17 look over

18 bring together

19 get lost

20 be expected to V

21 put out

정답
01 A에서 B까지 걸쳐 있다
02 ~에 영향을 미치다
03 ~에 관하여
04 당분간
05 사라지다
06 A가 B하는 것을 막다
07 간단히 말하면
08 ~을 조사하다
09 ~에 의존하다

10 나타나다
11 ~을 알고 있다
12 ~을 조립하다
13 끝나다
14 ~을 좋아하다
15 A뿐만 아니라 B 또한
16 며칠 전에
17 ~을 검토하다
18 ~을 합치다

19 길을 잃다
20 ~라고 예상되다
21 불을 끄다

Review Test

☑ 다음 숙어의 뜻을 우리말로 쓰시오.

01 look over _____

02 be expected to V _____

03 put out _____

04 bring together _____

05 get lost _____

06 for the time being _____

07 as to _____

08 be dependent on _____

09 be over _____

10 fade away _____

11 stop A from B(-ing) _____

12 be acquainted with _____

13 have an influence on _____

14 put together _____

15 the other day _____

16 range from A to B _____

17 show up _____

18 be fond of _____

19 in short _____

20 inquire into _____

21 not only A but (also) B _____

정답
01 ~을 검토하다
02 ~라고 예상되다
03 불을 끄다
04 ~을 합치다
05 길을 잃다
06 당분간
07 ~에 관하여
08 ~에 의존하다
09 끝나다

10 사라지다
11 A가 B하는 것을 막다
12 ~을 알고 있다
13 ~에 영향을 미치다
14 ~을 조립하다
15 며칠 전에
16 A에서 B까지 걸쳐 있다
17 나타나다
18 ~을 좋아하다

19 간단히 말하면
20 ~을 조사하다
21 A뿐만 아니라 B 또한

736	
vote for	찬성표를 던지다

737	
as a rule	대체로

738	
in respect of	~에 관하여

739	
hand out	~을 나눠 주다

740	
get caught up with	~에 사로잡히다

741	
mistake A for B	A를 B로 착각하다

742	
urge A to B	A가 B하도록 촉구하다

743	go about	~을 시작하다
744	fall asleep	잠들다
745	more or less	다소
746	bump into	우연히 마주치다
747	every other day	이틀마다
748	with the exception of	~을 제외하고
749	take a risk	위험을 무릅쓰다

750	
stand up for	~을 지지하다

751	
be located in	~에 위치해 있다

752	
be ignorant of	~을 모르다

753	
put ~ on hold	~을 잠시 중단하다

754	
take notes	필기하다

755	
look around	주위를 둘러보다

756	
take ~ for granted	~을 당연한 것으로 여기다

☑ 다음 숙어의 뜻을 우리말로 쓰시오.

01 look around _____

02 put ~ on hold _____

03 more or less _____

04 vote for _____

05 mistake A for B _____

06 go about _____

07 be ignorant of _____

08 in respect of _____

09 hand out _____

10 bump into _____

11 fall asleep _____

12 be located in _____

13 every other day _____

14 stand up for _____

15 take a risk _____

16 as a rule _____

17 take ~ for granted _____

18 urge A to B _____

19 take notes _____

20 get caught up with _____

21 with the exception of _____

정답			
	01 주위를 둘러보다	10 우연히 마주치다	19 필기하다
	02 ~을 잠시 중단하다	11 잠들다	20 ~에 사로잡히다
	03 다소	12 ~에 위치해 있다	21 ~을 제외하고
	04 찬성표를 던지다	13 이틀마다	
	05 A를 B로 착각하다	14 ~을 지지하다	
	06 ~을 시작하다	15 위험을 무릅쓰다	
	07 ~을 모르다	16 대체로	
	08 ~에 관하여	17 ~을 당연한 것으로 여기다	
	09 ~을 나눠 주다	18 A가 B하도록 촉구하다	

Review Test

☑ 다음 숙어의 뜻을 우리말로 쓰시오.

01 get caught up with _____

02 go about _____

03 hand out _____

04 take a risk _____

05 more or less _____

06 be located in _____

07 with the exception of _____

08 be ignorant of _____

09 put ~ on hold _____

10 mistake A for B _____

11 stand up for _____

12 in respect of _____

13 vote for _____

14 urge A to B _____

15 take ~ for granted _____

16 take notes _____

17 bump into _____

18 as a rule _____

19 fall asleep _____

20 every other day _____

21 look around _____

정답
01 ~에 사로잡히다
02 ~을 시작하다
03 ~을 나눠 주다
04 위험을 무릅쓰다
05 다소
06 ~에 위치해 있다
07 ~을 제외하고
08 ~을 모르다
09 ~을 잠시 중단하다

10 A를 B로 착각하다
11 ~을 지지하다
12 ~에 관하여
13 찬성표를 던지다
14 A가 B하도록 촉구하다
15 ~을 당연한 것으로 여기다
16 필기하다
17 우연히 마주치다
18 대체로

19 잠들다
20 이틀마다
21 주위를 둘러보다

Review Test

☑ 다음 숙어의 뜻을 우리말로 쓰시오.

01 fall asleep _____

02 be located in _____

03 put ~ on hold _____

04 take a risk _____

05 more or less _____

06 urge A to B _____

07 stand up for _____

08 take ~ for granted _____

09 get caught up with _____

10 vote for _____

11 with the exception of _____

12 in respect of _____

13 bump into _____

14 mistake A for B _____

15 go about _____

16 look around _____

17 as a rule _____

18 take notes _____

19 be ignorant of _____

20 every other day _____

21 hand out _____

정답 01 잠들다
      02 ~에 위치해 있다
      03 ~을 잠시 중단하다
      04 위험을 무릅쓰다
      05 다소
      06 A가 B하도록 촉구하다
      07 ~을 지지하다
      08 ~을 당연한 것으로 여기다
      09 ~에 사로잡히다

      10 찬성표를 던지다
      11 ~을 제외하고
      12 ~에 관하여
      13 우연히 마주치다
      14 A를 B로 착각하다
      15 ~을 시작하다
      16 주위를 둘러보다
      17 대체로
      18 필기하다

      19 ~을 모르다
      20 이틀마다
      21 ~을 나눠 주다

757	
keep on ~ing	계속해서 ~하다

758	
hold up	~을 떠받치다

759	
in the first place	우선

760	
under pressure	압박을 받는

761	
not less than	적어도

762	
take up	~을 차지하다

763	
from scratch	처음부터

764	
make an appointment	약속하다

765	
result from	~에서 비롯되다

766	
as is often the case	흔히 그렇듯이

767	
be aimed at	~을 목표로 하다

768	
in case	~의 경우에는

769	
free of charge	무료로

770	
run across	우연히 만나다

771	
be entitled to V	~할 자격이 있다

772	
make it a rule to V	~하는 것을 규칙으로 하다

773	
set up	~을 시작하다

774	
make a noise	시끄럽게 하다

775	
trick ~ into ...	~을 속여 ...하게 하다

776	
pull out	~을 꺼내다

777	
by far	훨씬

Review Test

☑ 다음 숙어의 뜻을 우리말로 쓰시오.

01 by far _____

02 set up _____

03 from scratch _____

04 run across _____

05 under pressure _____

06 keep on ~ing _____

07 pull out _____

08 trick ~ into ... _____

09 as is often the case _____

10 result from _____

11 make an appointment _____

12 be entitled to V _____

13 be aimed at _____

14 free of charge _____

15 not less than _____

16 take up _____

17 hold up _____

18 make it a rule to V _____

19 in the first place _____

20 make a noise _____

21 in case _____

정답
01 훨씬
02 ~을 시작하다
03 처음부터
04 우연히 만나다
05 압박을 받는
06 계속해서 ~하다
07 ~을 꺼내다
08 ~을 속여 ...하게 하다
09 흔히 그렇듯이

10 ~에서 비롯되다
11 약속하다
12 ~할 자격이 있다
13 ~을 목표로 하다
14 무료로
15 적어도
16 ~을 차지하다
17 ~을 떠받치다
18 ~하는 것을 규칙으로 하다

19 우선
20 시끄럽게 하다
21 ~의 경우에는

Review Test

☑ 다음 숙어의 뜻을 우리말로 쓰시오.

01 run across _____

02 keep on ~ing _____

03 as is often the case _____

04 make it a rule to V _____

05 from scratch _____

06 free of charge _____

07 hold up _____

08 not less than _____

09 trick ~ into ... _____

10 be entitled to V _____

11 in case _____

12 make an appointment _____

13 by far _____

14 result from _____

15 set up _____

16 be aimed at _____

17 take up _____

18 under pressure _____

19 in the first place _____

20 pull out _____

21 make a noise _____

정답
01 우연히 만나다
02 계속해서 ~하다
03 흔히 그렇듯이
04 ~하는 것을 규칙으로 하다
05 처음부터
06 무료로
07 ~을 떠받치다
08 적어도
09 ~을 속여 ...하게 하다
10 ~할 자격이 있다
11 ~의 경우에는
12 약속하다
13 훨씬
14 ~에서 비롯되다
15 ~을 시작하다
16 ~을 목표로 하다
17 ~을 차지하다
18 압박을 받는
19 우선
20 ~을 꺼내다
21 시끄럽게 하다

Review Test

☑ 다음 숙어의 뜻을 우리말로 쓰시오.

01 make an appointment

02 run across

03 make a noise

04 result from

05 under pressure

06 free of charge

07 be entitled to V

08 take up

09 from scratch

10 in case

11 as is often the case

12 trick ~ into ...

13 by far

14 not less than

15 be aimed at

16 keep on ~ing

17 in the first place

18 set up

19 make it a rule to V

20 hold up

21 pull out

정답
01 약속하다
02 우연히 만나다
03 시끄럽게 하다
04 ~에서 비롯되다
05 압박을 받는
06 무료로
07 ~할 자격이 있다
08 ~을 차지하다
09 처음부터

10 ~의 경우에는
11 흔히 그렇듯이
12 ~을 속여 ...하게 하다
13 훨씬
14 적어도
15 ~을 목표로 하다
16 계속해서 ~하다
17 우선
18 ~을 시작하다

19 ~하는 것을 규칙으로 하다
20 ~을 떠받치다
21 ~을 꺼내다

778

A bad workman always blames his tools.
서툰 일꾼이 장비만 탓한다.

779

A bird in the hand is worth two in a bush.
손 안의 새 한 마리가 숲 속에 있는 두 마리 새보다 낫다.

780

A burnt child dreads the fire.
불에 데어본 아이는 불을 무서워한다.

781

A crow is never whiter for washing herself often.
까마귀는 자주 씻는다고 더 하얗게 되지 않는다.

782

A drowning man will catch at a straw.
물에 빠진 사람은 지푸라기라도 잡는다.

783

A falling drop at last will cave a stone.
낙숫물이 바위를 뚫는다.

784

A friend in need is a friend indeed.
어려울 때의 친구가 진짜 친구이다.

785

A good beginning makes a good ending.

시작이 좋으면 끝도 좋다.

786

A good neighbor is better than a brother far off.

좋은 이웃은 멀리 떨어진 형제보다 낫다.

787

A journey of a thousand miles begins with a single step.

천리 길도 한 걸음부터.

788

A little is better than none.

조금이라도 있는 것이 없는 것보다는 낫다.

789

A little knowledge is dangerous.

얕팍한 지식은 위험하다.

790

A man is known by the company he keeps.

친구를 보면 그 사람을 안다.

791

A monkey sometimes falls from the tree.

원숭이도 때로는 나무에서 떨어지는 법이다.

792

A rolling stone gathers no moss.
구르는 돌에는 이끼가 끼지 않는다.

793

A small leak will sink a great ship.
조그만 구멍이 거대한 배를 침몰시키는 법이다.

794

A sound mind in a sound body.
건강한 신체에 건강한 마음이 깃든다.

795

A stitch in time saves nine.
제 때의 바느질 한 땀이 아홉 땀의 수고를 덜어준다.

796

A tree is known by its fruit.
열매를 보면 그 나무를 안다.

797

A trouble shared is a trouble split in half.
고통은 나누면 반으로 줄어든다.

798

A watched pot never boils.
서두른다고 일이 되는 것은 아니다.

799

Actions speak louder than words.

말보다 행동이 앞선다.

800

All is well that ends well.

끝이 좋아야 다 좋다.

801

All that glitters is not gold.

반짝인다고 해서 모두 다 금인 것은 아니다.

802

Always put yourself in the other person's shoes.

다른 사람의 입장에서 생각하라.

803

An early bird catches the worm.

일찍 일어나는 새가 벌레를 잡는다.

804

As the twig is bent, so grows the tree.

될 성 싶은 나무는 떡잎부터 알아본다.

805

As you sow, so shall you reap.

뿌린 대로 거둔다.

Review Test

☑ 다음 속담의 뜻을 우리말로 쓰시오.

01. A good neighbor is better than a brother far off.

02. A small leak will sink a great ship.

03. All that glitters is not gold.

04. A bird in the hand is worth two in a bush.

05. A burnt child dreads the fire.

06. A trouble shared is a trouble split in half.

07. An early bird catches the worm.

정답 01. 좋은 이웃은 멀리 떨어진 형제보다 낫다.　　05. 불에 데어본 아이는 불을 무서워한다.

02. 조그만 구멍이 거대한 배를 침몰시키는 법이다.　　06. 고통은 나누면 반으로 줄어든다.

03. 반짝인다고 해서 모두 다 금인 것은 아니다.　　07. 일찍 일어나는 새가 벌레를 잡는다.

04. 손 안의 새 한 마리가 숲 속에 있는 두 마리 새보다 낫다.

☑ 다음 속담의 뜻을 우리말로 쓰시오.

08. A bad workman always blames his tools.

09. A friend in need is a friend indeed.

10. A crow is never whiter for washing herself often.

11. A little is better than none.

12. Always put yourself in the other person's shoes.

13. A monkey sometimes falls from the tree.

14. A man is known by the company he keeps.

정답 | 08. 서툰 일꾼이 장비만 탓한다. | 12. 다른 사람의 입장에서 생각하라.

09. 어려울 때의 친구가 진짜 친구이다. | 13. 원숭이도 때로는 나무에서 떨어지는 법이다.

10. 까마귀는 자주 씻는다고 더 하얗게 되지 않는다. | 14. 친구를 보면 그 사람을 안다.

11. 조금이라도 있는 것이 없는 것보다는 낫다.

Review Test

☑ 다음 속담의 뜻을 우리말로 쓰시오.

15. All is well that ends well.

16. Actions speak louder than words.

17. A watched pot never boils.

18. As you sow, so shall you reap.

19. A rolling stone gathers no moss.

20. A good beginning makes a good ending.

21. A stitch in time saves nine.

정답 15. 끝이 좋아야 다 좋다.   19. 구르는 돌에는 이끼가 끼지 않는다.

16. 말보다 행동이 앞선다.   20. 시작이 좋으면 끝도 좋다.

17. 서두른다고 일이 되는 것은 아니다.   21. 제때의 바느질 한 땀이 아홉 땀의 수고를 덜어준다.

18. 뿌린 대로 거둔다.

Review Test

☑ 다음 속담의 뜻을 우리말로 쓰시오.

22.   As the twig is bent, so grows the tree.

23.   A little knowledge is dangerous.

24.   A falling drop at last will cave a stone.

25.   A journey of a thousand miles begins with a single step.

26.   A drowning man will catch at a straw.

27.   A sound mind in a sound body.

28.   A tree is known by its fruit.

DAY 39　속담

806

Attack is the best defence.
공격이 최선의 방어이다.

807

Bad news has wings.
나쁜 소식은 빨리 퍼진다.

808

Behind the clouds is the sun still shining.
고생 끝에 낙이 온다.

809

Better late than never.
늦더라도 전혀 안하는 것보다 낫다.

810

Birds of a feather flock together.
깃이 같은 새는 끼리끼리 모인다.

811

By other's faults wise men correct their own.
현명한 사람은 남의 결점을 보고 자기의 결점을 고친다.

812

Clouds gather before a storm.
폭풍우 전에 구름이 모인다.

813

Curiosity kills the cat.
지나친 호기심은 위험한 법이다.

814

Do in Rome as the Romans do.
로마에서는 로마법을 따라라.

815

Do to others as you would be done by.
네가 대접받고 싶은 대로 남을 대접하라.

816

Don't bite off more than you can chew.
능력 밖의 일을 하려고 하지 마라.

817

Don't bite the hand that feeds you.
은혜를 원수로 갚지 마라.

818

Don't count your chickens before they are hatched.
병아리가 부화하기도 전에 미리 몇 마리인지 세지 말라.

819

Don't judge a book by its cover.
외모로 사람을 판단하지 마라.

820

Don't judge a man until you're walked in his boots.
그 사람의 처지가 되어 보기 전에 함부로 판단하지 말라.

821

Don't put the cart before the horse.
일의 순서를 거꾸로 뒤집지 말라.

822

Easier said than done.
말하기는 쉬워도 행동하기는 어렵다.

823

Empty vessels make the greatest noise.
빈 수레가 요란하다.

824

Every cloud has a silver lining.
하늘이 무너져도 솟아 날 구멍은 있다.

825

Every dog has his day.
쥐구멍에도 볕들 날이 있다.

826

Everything has its time.
모든 것은 다 때가 있다.

827

Good medicine tastes bitter.
좋은 약은 입에 쓰다.

828

Habit is a second nature.
습관은 고치기 어렵다.

829

Haste makes waste.
급히 서두르면 일을 망친다.

830

He laughs best who laughs last.
마지막에 웃는 자가 진정한 승자다.

831

He who makes no mistakes makes nothing.
누구나 실수를 하기 마련이다.

832

Heaven helps those who help themselves.
하늘은 스스로 돕는 자를 돕는다.

833

Honesty is the best policy.
정직이 최상의 방책이다.

Review Test ─────────────────

☑ 다음 속담의 뜻을 우리말로 쓰시오.

01. He who makes no mistakes makes nothing.

02. Good medicine tastes bitter.

03. Don't bite off more than you can chew.

04. He laughs best who laughs last.

05. Everything has its time.

06. Easier said than done.

07. Clouds gather before a storm.

정답　01. 누구나 실수를 하기 마련이다.　　　05. 모든 것은 다 때가 있다.

02. 좋은 약은 입에 쓰다.　　　　　　　06. 말하기는 쉬워도 행동하기는 어렵다.

03. 능력 밖의 일을 하려고 하지 마라.　　07. 폭풍우 전에 구름이 모인다.

04. 마지막에 웃는 자가 진정한 승자다.

Review Test

☑ 다음 속담의 뜻을 우리말로 쓰시오.

08. Every cloud has a silver lining.

09. Bad news has wings.

10. Don't bite the hand that feeds you.

11. By other's faults wise men correct their own.

12. Do in Rome as the Romans do.

13. Birds of a feather flock together.

14. Haste makes waste.

정답   08. 하늘이 무너져도 솟아 날 구멍은 있다.　　12. 로마에서는 로마법을 따라라.

09. 나쁜 소식은 빨리 퍼진다.　　13. 깃이 같은 새는 끼리끼리 모인다.

10. 은혜를 원수로 갚지 마라.　　14. 급히 서두르면 일을 망친다.

11. 현명한 사람은 남의 결점을 보고 자기의 결점을 고친다.

Review Test

☑ 다음 속담의 뜻을 우리말로 쓰시오.

15. Curiosity kills the cat.

16. Behind the clouds is the sun still shining.

17. Empty vessels make the greatest noise.

18. Don't judge a man until you're walked in his boots.

19. Habit is a second nature.

20. Do to others as you would be done by.

21. Heaven helps those who help themselves.

정답 15. 지나친 호기심은 위험한 법이다.   19. 습관은 고치기 어렵다.

16. 고생 끝에 낙이 온다.   20. 네가 대접받고 싶은 대로 남을 대접하라.

17. 빈 수레가 요란하다.   21. 하늘은 스스로 돕는 자를 돕는다.

18. 그 사람의 처지가 되어 보기 전에 함부로 판단하지 말라.

238

☑ 다음 속담의 뜻을 우리말로 쓰시오.

22. Better late than never.

23. Honesty is the best policy.

24. Attack is the best defence.

25. Don't count your chickens before they are hatched.

26. Don't judge a book by its cover.

27. Every dog has his day.

28. Don't put the cart before the horse.

정답   22. 늦더라도 전혀 안하는 것보다 낫다.

26. 외모로 사람을 판단하지 마라.

23. 정직이 최상의 방책이다.

27. 쥐구멍에도 볕들 날이 있다.

24. 공격이 최선의 방어이다.

28. 일의 순서를 거꾸로 뒤집지 마라.

25. 병아리가 부화하기도 전에 미리 몇 마리인지 세지 말라.

834

It is no use crying over spilt milk.
이미 지나간 일을 후회해도 소용없다.

835

It never rains but it pours.
불행은 겹친다.

836

It's never too late to learn.
배움에 나이는 없다.

837

Knowledge is power.
아는 것이 힘이다.

838

Lend your money and lose your friend.
돈을 빌려주면 친구를 잃는다.

839

Let bygones be bygones.
지난 일은 지난 일인 채로 두어라.

840

Little pot is soon hot.
그릇이 작은 사람일수록 쉽게 화를 낸다.

841

Look before you leap.
돌다리도 두드려 보고 건너라.

842

Make haste slowly.
급할수록 천천히

843

Make hay while the sun shines.
기회를 놓치지 마라.

844

Many a little makes a mickle.
작은 것들이 모여서 거대한 것을 이룬다.

845

Necessity is the mother of invention.
필요는 발명의 어머니.

846

Never put off till tomorrow what you can do today.
오늘 할 일을 내일로 미루지 말라.

847

No pains, no gains.
노력하지 않으면 얻는 것도 없다.

848

No rule without exception.
예외없는 규칙은 없다.

849

No smoke without fire.
아니 땐 굴뚝에 연기 나랴.

850

Nothing ventured, nothing gained.
세상에 저절로 얻어지는 것은 없다.

851

One cannot see the wood for the trees.
나무만 보고 숲은 보지 못한다.

852

One hour today is worth two tomorrow.
오늘의 한 시간은 내일의 두 시간의 가치가 있다.

853

One man's meat is another man's poison.
어떤 사람에게는 약이 다른 사람에게는 독이 될 수도 있다.

854

One picture is worth a thousand words.
백문이 불여일견.

855

Opportunity seldom knocks twice.
기회는 쉽게 찾아오지 않는다.

856

Out of sight, out of mind.
눈에서 멀어지면 마음에서도 멀어진다.

857

Plow deep while sluggards sleep.
게으름뱅이들이 잠자는 동안 밭을 열심히 갈아라.

858

Prevention is better than cure.
예방이 치료보다 낫다.

859

Rome was not built in a day.
로마는 하루아침에 이루어지지 않는다.

860

Saying is one thing and doing another.
말하는 것과 직접 행동하는 것은 별개의 문제다.

861

Slow and steady wins the race.
느려도 착실히 하면 이긴다.

Review Test

☑ 다음 속담의 뜻을 우리말로 쓰시오.

01. Nothing ventured, nothing gained

02. Out of sight, out of mind.

03. Plow deep while sluggards sleep.

04. One man's meat is another man's poison.

05. Let bygones be bygones.

06. Make haste slowly.

07. One cannot see the wood for the trees.

정답   01. 세상에 저절로 얻어지는 것은 없다.   05. 지난일은 지난일인 채로 두어라.

02. 눈에서 멀어지면 마음에서도 멀어진다.   06. 급할수록 천천히

03. 게으름뱅이들이 잠자는 동안 밭을 열심히 갈아라.   07. 나무만 보고 숲은 보지 못한다.

04. 어떤 사람에게는 약이 다른 사람에게는 독이 될 수도 있다.

☑ 다음 속담의 뜻을 우리말로 쓰시오.

08. Slow and steady wins the race.

09. Rome was not built in a day.

10. Little pot is soon hot.

11. One picture is worth a thousand words.

12. Make hay while the sun shines.

13. No pains, no gains.

14. Necessity is the mother of invention.

정답   08. 느려도 착실히 하면 이긴다.   12. 기회를 놓치지 마라.

09. 로마는 하루아침에 이루어지지 않는다.   13. 노력하지 않으면 얻는 것도 없다.

10. 그릇이 작은 사람일수록 쉽게 화를 낸다.   14. 필요는 발명의 어머니.

11. 백문이 불여일견.

Review Test ─────────────────

☑ 다음 속담의 뜻을 우리말로 쓰시오.

15. Lend your money and lose your friend.

16. Prevention is better than cure.

17. No rule without exception.

18. No smoke without fire.

19. Never put off till tomorrow what you can do today.

20. It is no use crying over spilt milk.

21. Look before you leap.

정답 15. 돈을 빌려주면 친구를 잃는다.   19. 오늘 할 일을 내일로 미루지 말라.

16. 예방이 치료보다 낫다.   20. 이미 지나간 일을 후회해도 소용없다.

17. 예외없는 규칙은 없다.   21. 돌다리도 두드려 보고 건너라.

18. 아니 땐 굴뚝에 연기 나랴.

☑ 다음 속담의 뜻을 우리말로 쓰시오.

22. Opportunity seldom knocks twice.

23. It never rains but it pours.

24. Saying is one thing and doing another.

25. Many a little makes a mickle.

26. Knowledge is power.

27. One hour today is worth two tomorrow.

28. It's never too late to learn.

정답   22. 기회는 쉽게 찾아오지 않는다.   26. 아는 것이 힘이다.

23. 불행은 겹친다.   27. 오늘의 한 시간은 내일의 두 시간의 가치가 있다.

24. 말하는 것과 직접 행동하는 것은 별개의 문제다.   28. 배움에 나이는 없다.

25. 작은 것들이 모여서 거대한 것을 이룬다.

862

So many men, so many minds.
사람마다 생각이 다 다르다.

863

Soon got, soon gone.
쉽게 얻은 것은 쉽게 나간다.

864

Spare the rod and spoil the child.
매를 아끼면 아이를 망친다.

865

Still waters run deep.
빈 수레가 요란하다.

866

Strike while the iron is hot.
쇠는 뜨거울 때 두드려라.

867

The darkest hour is that before the dawn.
새벽이 오기 직전이 가장 어둡다.

868

The foot of the candle is dark.
등잔 밑이 어둡다.

869

The grass always greener on the other side.

남의 떡이 더 커 보인다.

870

The leopard does not change his spots.

세 살 버릇 여든까지 간다.

871

The more, the better.

많으면 많을수록 좋다.

872

The pen is mightier than the sword.

펜은 칼보다 강하다.

873

The whole is more than the sum of its parts.

여럿이 모이면 각각의 합보다 더 큰 결과를 만든다.

874

There is no rose without a thorn.

모든 장미에는 가시가 있다.

875

Time and tide wait for no man.

세월은 사람을 기다려 주지 않는다.

876

Time flies like an arrow.
시간은 화살처럼 빠르게 흐른다.

877

Time heals all wounds.
시간은 모든 것을 치료한다.

878

Time will show who is right.
누가 옳은지는 시간이 보여줄 것이다.

879

Too many cooks spoil the broth.
사공이 많으면 배가 산으로 간다.

880

Two heads are better than one.
백지장도 맞들면 낫다.

881

Walls have ears.
낮 말은 새가 듣고 밤 말은 쥐가 듣는다.

882

Well begun is half done.
시작이 반이다.

883

What the fool does at last, the wise man does at first.
바보들이 맨 마지막에 하는 일을 현명한 사람들은 제일 먼저 한다.

884

When one door shuts, another opens.
기회는 항상 있다.

885

Where there is a will, there is a way.
뜻이 있는 곳에 길이 있다.

886

Who knows most speaks least.
현명한 사람은 지혜를 뽐내지 않는다.

887

You can't have your cake and eat it too.
두 가지를 동시에 가질 수는 없다.

888

You don't know what you've got until you've lost it.
잃어버리기 전까지는 스스로가 가진 것이 무엇인지를 모른다.

889

You win some, you lose some.
얻는 것이 있으면 잃는 것도 있다.

Review Test

☑ 다음 속담의 뜻을 우리말로 쓰시오.

01. Time flies like an arrow.

02. Who knows most speaks least.

03. Time and tide wait for no man.

04. What the fool does at last, the wise man does at first.

05. The foot of the candle is dark.

06. The darkest hour is that before the dawn.

07. The whole is more than the sum of its parts.

정답   01. 시간은 화살처럼 빠르게 흐른다.   05. 등잔밑이 어둡다.

02. 현명한 사람은 지혜를 뽐내지 않는다.   06. 새벽이 오기 직전이 가장 어둡다.

03. 세월은 사람을 기다려 주지 않는다.   07. 여럿이 모이면 각각의 합보다 더 큰 결과를 만든다.

04. 바보들이 맨 마지막에 하는 일을 현명한 사람들은 제일 먼저 한다.

☑ 다음 속담의 뜻을 우리말로 쓰시오.

08. Where there is a will, there is a way.

09. The leopard does not change his spots.

10. The pen is mightier than the sword.

11. You don't know what you've got until you've lost it.

12. Two heads are better than one.

13. There is no rose without a thorn.

14. The more, the better.

정답 08. 뜻이 있는 곳에 길이 있다.   12. 백지장도 맞들면 낫다.

09. 세 살 버릇 여든까지 간다.   13. 모든 장미에는 가시가 있다.

10. 펜은 칼보다 강하다.   14. 많으면 많을수록 좋다.

11. 잃어버리기 전까지는 스스로가 가진 것이 무엇인지를 모른다.

Review Test ————————————————

15. When one door shuts, another opens.

16. Still waters run deep.

17. Soon got, soon gone.

18. Spare the rod and spoil the child.

19. The grass always greener on the other side.

20. Too many cooks spoil the broth.

21. Well begun is half done.

정답 15. 기회는 항상 있다.   19. 남의 떡이 더 커 보인다.

16. 빈 수레가 요란하다.   20. 사공이 많으면 배가 산으로 간다.

17. 쉽게 얻은 것은 쉽게 나간다.   21. 시작이 반이다.

18. 매를 아끼면 아이를 망친다.

☑ 다음 속담의 뜻을 우리말로 쓰시오.

22. Time will show who is right.

23. Time heals all wounds.

24. Strike while the iron is hot.

25. You can't have your cake and eat it too.

26. So many men, so many minds.

27. Walls have ears.

28. You win some, you lose some.

정답 22. 누가 옳은지는 시간이 보여줄 것이다.

26. 사람마다 생각이 다 다르다.

23. 시간은 모든 것을 치료한다.

27. 낮 말은 새가 듣고 밤 말은 쥐가 듣는다.

24. 쇠는 뜨거울 때 두드려라.

28. 얻는 것이 있으면 잃는 것도 있다.

25. 두 가지를 동시에 가질 수는 없다.

Premium Voca 숙어 + 속담 편

발　행 | 2024년 06월 14일
저　자 | 영어중심
펴낸이 | 한건희
펴낸곳 | 주식회사 부크크
출판사등록 | 2014.07.15.(제2014-16호)
주　소 | 서울특별시 금천구 가산디지털1로 119 SK트윈타워 A동
　　　　305호
전　화 | 1670-8316
이메일 | info@bookk.co.kr

ISBN | 979-11-410-8952-8

www.bookk.co.kr
ⓒ 영어중심 2024